Upper Room
on Main Street

‑»»«‑

Upper Room
on Main Street

>>‖ *by* ‖<<

HAROLD BLAKE WALKER

Harper & Brothers • Publishers
New York

Library of Congress catalog card number: 53–10981

To My Mother

CONTENTS

7

FOREWORD

WILLIAM COWPER, WHO PAINTED AN OMINOUS WORD PICTURE OF his own times, might have been writing of our day when he described a world

> . . . . that seems
> To toll the death bell of its own decease,
> And by the voice of all its elements
> To preach the general doom.

Crisis, it is apparent, is a perpetual element in human affairs. However, if we are tempted to take comfort from the fact that others have faced crises, it should be noted that there is a pyramiding of crises in history, with crisis piled on crisis. Critical issues blunderingly met and problems whose solution is postponed add fury to their successors until we come to a time when, as General MacArthur noted, "We have had our last chance."

The impounded fury of a muddled past is ranged against us now as we seek to build a "brave new world." Our sins have found us out. We face the future anxiously and the present with misgivings. We have created the power with which to destroy ourselves. At such a time a minister is constrained to examine his ministry and to wonder if preaching is an adequate instrument with which to meet the contemporary challenge to civilization. Can preaching save the world? The question is by no means merely academic. It is frightfully important. Can preaching change human character enough to save humanity from the agony of a new dark age? I often wonder. And yet, in the moments when I am disturbed by grave doubts, I am haunted by the word of St. Paul, that "it pleased God by the foolishness of preaching to save them that believe."

It is the business of preaching to make words the instrument and the servant of saving ideas. It is no light trust the preacher bears. He has twenty-five or thirty minutes to wield the weapon of words, a half hour to say only essential things, a fragment of time to crack the sky and let God through. He has a handful of minutes to silence the tempest in the souls of men, pierce their preoccupation with the things of the world, and penetrate their minds with shafts of light. He has no time for the trivial. There is so little time.

Obviously the preacher does not speak for himself. He is no merchant of words casting about for a theme. He is not an after-dinner speaker intent on entertaining a crowd. He is a custodian of eternal ideas wrought in the suffering and death of Calvary and sublimely confirmed in the resurrection of Easter dawn. His excuse for being is in the admonition, "preach the word"—not his own word, not the world's word, but God's word. "Prepare ye the way of the Lord" is the essence of his charter and the character of his task.

These sermons were preached from the pulpit of the First Presbyterian Church of Evanston in an effort to bring the resources of the Christian faith to bear upon the everyday problems of ordinary people, living in a time of insecurity and peril. They seek to relate the Christian ethic and the Christian hope to the personal and social problems of our time in the faith that the gospel is timeless and its resources adequate to bear the strain of living in such a time as this.

I am grateful to my secretary, Mrs. Ella Coninx, for her careful preparation of the manuscript, to the congregation of the First Presbyterian Church, whose loyalty and encouragement have been an inspiration, and to my wife, whose patience and constructive criticism have been a constant resource.

For permission to quote copyrighted material I am indebted to the following: Musette Publishers, Inc., for the poem *Labor* by Langston Hughes; Harcourt, Brace and Company, Inc. for the quotation from *The Cocktail Party* by T. S. Eliot; Samuel French, Ltd. for the lines from *A Prayer* by John Drinkwater; and Dodd, Mead & Company, Inc. for the lines from *Complete Poems* by Paul Laurence Dunbar.

HAROLD BLAKE WALKER

First Presbyterian Church
Evanston, Illinois

You and I and God

-»>«<-

    I go to prove my soul!
I see my way as birds their trackless way.
I shall arrive! what time, what circuit first,
I ask not; but unless God send his hail
Or blinding fire-balls, sleet or stifling snow,
In some time, His good time, I shall arrive:
He guides me and the bird. In his good time.
            Robert Browning, "Paracelsus"

WHEN GOD SAYS "NO"

For this thing I besought the Lord thrice, that it might
depart from me.   II CORINTHIANS 12:8

IT IS SIGNIFICANT TO OBSERVE THAT THE GREATEST OF ALL CHRISTIAN
missionaries was a man who through all his days bore a physical
affliction. He had what he called "a thorn in the flesh." Joseph
Klausner, great Jewish scholar, thinks Paul was an epileptic. There
are other scholars who insist he suffered from persistent malaria,
still others who think he had arthritis. In any case, Paul was a constant sufferer and he was troubled. He was giving his life for his
Lord, and it seemed only reasonable that God should take away his
infirmity. So, as Paul wrote the Corinthian church, "For this thing
I besought the Lord thrice, that it might depart from me." Nevertheless, saint though he was, Paul carried his affliction to the grave.
So much the record makes clear.

I

Obviously, Paul was no spiritual neophyte. He was a spiritual
giant. He wrote more of the New Testament than any other man.
He started more churches than any single man before or since. He
laid the foundations for Christian theology. He endured persecution
and risked death a dozen times for the sake of the gospel of Christ.
But despite all that, God said "No" when Paul prayed to be relieved

of his affliction. Paul went on suffering and serving to the end of his days. A lesser man would have said it was not fair, or else assumed he needed a new technique to persuade the reluctance of God. It was not so with Paul. He took his pain in his stride saying: "Most gladly . . . will I glory in my infirmities, that the power of Christ may rest upon me."

Like Paul we may as well face the fact that there are times when God says "No" to our petitions however ardently they are uttered. Who can forget the prayer of Jesus in the garden of Gethsemane as the sweat stood out on his forehead: "Let this cup pass from me?" Suffering and death awaited Jesus and in the agony of the hour he prayed to be saved. But God said "No." And without that terrible "No" there would have been no Easter, no shining crosses now to stir the dull world's soul. Without that awful "No" in the garden there would have been no light beyond the dark.

Still we are resentful when our skies tumble in with God's thundering "No." Like Martin Luther we shout in our petulant rage: "My God, art thou dead?" In our frustration we turn our backs upon God and cease to believe in Him. If God will not do what we want done, what's the use of having faith? If prayer does not get us what we want, what's the use of praying? As one woman said to her pastor: "I have been praying incessantly for God to heal my sick son. If He does not do something soon I will lose my faith in Him." Our unbelief, you see, is mostly a matter of psychological frustration.

Where we go wrong is in the naïve feeling that by way of Christian faith and ardent prayer we should become perfectly healthy, wealthy and popular. But, as the old song has it: "It ain't necessarily so." Indeed, most of the saints were not physically robust. St. Francis of Assisi had tuberculosis, and St. Loyola was a cripple from the ravages of war. God said "No" to their pleas for healing. Most of God's saints have been poor. Indeed, I cannot think of a saint in all history who got rich being a saint. What is more, most of the saints were unpopular. Savonarola was burned at the stake, and John Huss and John Wycliffe suffered the same fate. So far as I can discover, there is nothing in the New Testament anywhere to suggest that Christian prayer, however devout, should make people completely healthy, wealthy or popular.

II

When God said "No" to Paul, the great apostle put two and two together and came up with the idea that his affliction could minister to his humility, as he said, "lest I be exalted above measure." Paul was eloquent and he was brilliant. He was a power in the early church, influential in its counsels. What is more, he had been a proud, unbending Pharisee, whose pride had gotten in the way of his spiritual insight and whose ego had jaundiced his perception of the will of God. Paul's "thorn in the flesh" served as a perpetual reminder of his spiritual need. He could not cure his affliction. Even Luke, the beloved physician who traveled so often with Paul, was impotent to heal his friend. No doubt Luke did what he could. So Paul faced the fact he would have to bear his "thorn in the flesh" and let "the power of Christ rest upon" him to see him through.

Throughout his days Paul's "thorn in the flesh" made him acutely aware of his need for strength beyond his own. Without "the power of Christ" he could not manage the pain, and he knew it. Without unceasing prayer he would have to take to his bed, and leave hard toil to the healthy. He understood full well what Jesus meant when he said: "Without me, ye can do nothing." He put his feeling plainly when he wrote: "I can do all things through Christ who strengtheneth me." On his own, he was whipped, with Christ, he was "more than conqueror."

Paul sensed the simple fact that we cannot be helped until we are humbled. What is more he knew that humility is a difficult virtue when we are riding the crest of the wave. Healthy, wealthy and popular, we get along nicely without God, at least so it appears. In our self-sufficient arrogance we suspect that prayer is a device for the weak who cannot handle life by themselves. We have what it takes to make a go of life, and what can God do for us that we cannot do for ourselves with our wits and courage? We can run our business, support our families and get by very nicely, thank you, without bothering God. Let the weak lean on "the everlasting arms," we will just take a little aspirin for our headaches when we have them.

Like as not we have to meet something we cannot manage before we get around to prayer and a decent reverence for God. We seldom look for help until we know we need it to survive. The student does not seek help with his studies until he knows that without it he will fail. He needed help all along, but he was too proud to admit it even to himself. The alcoholic cannot be helped until he knows he is finished without assistance from beyond himself. Usually he has to hit bottom before he can climb back with the help of Alcoholics Anonymous and God. The world is full of maladjusted people too proud to ask for help, so they blunder on to their miserable destiny. They will not look for help until they know they are lost without it.

Often we are like the man who was seen racing down a country road, running desperately to catch a train. He almost made it; but not quite. Panting at the station gate, he looked miserably at the stationmaster, who remarked most unhelpfully: "Son, you just didn't start soon enough!" So it is with most of us. We get along nicely until we meet something we cannot manage, and then we discover we are totally unprepared to manage disaster and disappointment. We did not start soon enough to be ready for the unmanageable. We are left, quite miserably on the station platform watching life go on without us.

Self-sufficient in health and economic plenty we do not bother about prayer, and then all unsuspecting we meet the unmanageable.

It is a blow to our pride and like as not we rebel. "It isn't fair," we say petulantly, as if the God we utterly forgot should have kept us in mind. Of course, He has had us in mind all along, but we did not bother to find out about the love that never lets us go. We thought we did not need God. Then we met sickness or shattering sorrow or desperate failure, and learned the sober truth that we always needed God, never more than when we thought we were strong enough by ourselves.

Paul knew himself better than most men. Maybe that is why he thought he needed his "thorn in the flesh" to keep him humble and responsive to the power of Christ. He might have gone off on a tangent, proud of himself and his accomplishments, and a bit condescending toward God. In any event, it is clear from the record that Paul looked upon his "thorn in the flesh" as a physical handicap that brought with it a spiritual blessing.

III

Certainly God's "No" to Paul's plea for healing was not a bare "No." God never says "No" to our pleas, like tired parents who mean they do not wish to be bothered further. There is always a "Yea" that is linked to the "Nay," a road that is open beside the one that is closed. If there isn't full healing, at least there is help, and often some healing in the help. Paul found it so, for God's "No" ended with an affirmation: "My grace is sufficient for thee; for my strength is made perfect in weakness." Though Paul could not be fully healed, he could have a compensating spiritual gift.

The author of the 73rd Psalm felt the truth when he considered his suffering and his tragic exile too. "My flesh and my heart faileth," he wrote, "but God is the strength of my heart, and my portion for ever." Sick and homeless, yes, but still strong in God. Such was the experience of Katherine Mansfield, the gifted author who died in 1922 at the age of thirty-four, after a long struggle with disease. She wrote in her journal: "I should like this to be accepted as my confession. There is no limit to human suffering. When one thinks: 'Now I have touched the bottom of the sea—now I can go no deeper, one does go deeper.' I do not want to die without leaving a record of my belief that suffering can be overcome. For I do believe it. What must one do? Do not resist. Take it. Be overwhelmed. Accept it fully. Make it a part of life. Everything in life that we really accept undergoes a change. So suffering must become love. . . . I must pass from personal love to greater love." And a little while later, pressing on through suffering to her work she wrote: "May I be found worthy to do it! Lord, make me crystal clear for Thy light to shine through."

So Paul accepted his "thorn in the flesh," and his suffering became love for mankind with the light of God shining through. So Katherine Mansfield accepted suffering, and her suffering became love, crystal clear for the light of God to shine through. What is more, by way of that light, her husband, John Middleton Murry, an agnostic, saw so much of God that he embraced the Church of England. In one he loved dearly he saw the redeeming truth: "My grace is sufficient for thee, for my strength is made perfect in weakness." Let there be no mistake: Though there may be no healing, there always is help and power to use suffering creatively for the light of God to shine through.

Prayer in the face of our troubles or afflictions is not a matter of informing God of something He does not already know, or pleading with God to change His "No" to "Yes." Prayer is opening the soul to God so that He can point the way for us. "Prayer is not overcoming God's reluctance; it is laying hold of God's willingness." Paul gave up trying to overcome God's "No," and laid hold of God's "Yes." He listened for the answer to his plea for healing, and found it not in healing, but in help; not in cure but in creative courage. Out of the night of his pain came the word: "My strength is made perfect in weakness."

The trouble we meet in our prayers lies in our failure to lay hold of God's willingness after we have felt the frustration of His reluctance to do what we want done. Yet some of the noblest Christians I have known have been men and women who dared to believe God could take the leftovers of their broken bodies and disappointed hopes and use them gloriously. I remember a schoolteacher, laid low by an incurable illness, but for ten long years she has sat in her room while hundreds of her former students trudge to her door to leave their troubles there. Radiant and cheerful, she has found the power of God to lift the burdens of others, and to inspire their faith in God. Even preachers have found a ministry of hope in her spirit; a glowing evidence of the truths they preach. God said "No" to her prayer for healing so she laid hold of God's willingness and let Him take her life and use it as a bulwark for the souls of men to lean upon.

IV

There is one thing more that Paul learned when God said "No" to his prayer for healing. Said he: "When I am weak, then am I strong." His physical weakness became the source of his spiritual strength, and his spiritual strength overcame his physical affliction. I think G. A. Studdert-Kennedy, British poet and preacher, was the most striking illustration I ever saw of that truth. Years ago I heard him speak to some seven thousand young people at a convention in Indianapolis. His body was frail and emaciated, weakened by the ravages of tuberculosis, and he shuffled to the speaker's stand as if it were a gruesome effort. But when he spoke, there was an electric power in him, as if some hidden flame were burning bright. The light of God and the power of God used that frail, tortured body to stir seven thousand young people that day. In his weakness he was strong in the strength of God.

Such power does not just happen. Paul's strength in weakness did not just happen. It came from deep roots in the love and the goodness of God. You cannot pick strawberries from brambles, neither can you pick power from pessimism, or radiance from resentment. When God says "No" to what you want, remember that what you really need is not what you ask, but God Himself, His strength for your weakness; His grace in your disappointment. Some day maybe we shall learn that the more we pray the better things go and the less we pray the worse they go. The more we lay hold of God's willingness, the less we are disturbed by His reluctance. The more we claim God's strength, the less we are worried by our weakness.

But finding God's strength for our weakness is by no means a casual matter, a Sunday excursion when something else does not interfere. It is a daily business and it seldom pays off on a regular schedule. "Pray without ceasing," said Jesus, and the Psalmist adds a postscript: "If the vision tarry, wait for it." That is where we fail. Our prayers are mostly after-thoughts, not the common mood of every hour at work and at home. What is more, we have no wish to wait. As John Wesley noted: "The difference between God and me is that I am in a hurry and God is not." We want answers to our prayers at once, or else we just quit praying.

There is a hint of our mood in the comment of a lad at a young people's meeting. Said he: "Let's make the devotions snappy and get on with the program." So we want to be on with our program with no time to wait to lay hold of God's program for us. We want healing now, not tomorrow or the next day. We cannot manage to wait. It is only another illustration of the pride that keeps us from the power of God. We want to manage God and His will, God and His timetable. If He does not dance to our tune we won't believe in Him, and that's that.

Paul knew better. He spent a year in Arabia praying and thinking. Every letter he wrote breathed the spirit of prayer. He prayed on the roads he traveled, in the prisons where he waited, on the ships he sailed, in the homes where he paused. He knew he could manage his "thorn in the flesh" with God; but he could not carry on alone. He knew he could keep on with the strength of God girding his weakness. He could not keep going alone. So it is with you and with me. We can manage our ills with God, and keep sweet; but we are done on our own. We can take pain and hurt in our stride if we know God's "strength is made perfect in weakness."

SAILING UNDER SEALED ORDERS

Now the word of the Lord came unto Jonah, the son of
Amittai, saying, "Arise, go to Nineveh."   JONAH 1:1–2

IT IS A MAJOR MISFORTUNE THAT THE SPIRITUAL SIGNIFICANCE OF THE
book of Jonah has been obscured by a minor argument. I am
sure that the prophet who wrote the story would be greatly disturbed by the discovery that ecclesiastical minds had missed the
point and lost their perspective debating whether a whale could
manage to swallow Jonah. The insight of Jonah was deeply spiritual
and he said what he had to say by way of a story, a story with a
point which the ages have not dulled. Like Jesus, he used a parable
to preach a sermon.

Just consider the story. The "word of the Lord came unto Jonah
. . . saying, 'Arise, go to Nineveh.'" And of course God spoke to
Jonah as he speaks to us with the still small voice that says, "I
ought," "I must." Anybody could see that Nineveh needed a preacher.
The place was in a state of moral chaos. The merchants were dishonest, the government was corrupt and cruel, and as in ancient
Sodom, the people of the town were taking a moral vacation. Jonah
took one long-range look at Nineveh and said: "No thank you."
Then, to guard against any weakening that might send him to the

unholy city, he took ship for Tarshish. Like many of us, Jonah had the naïve idea that he could run away from his responsibility and escape the inward voice simply by changing his residence.

Unhappily for Jonah, his little ship nearly floundered in a wild sea, and the ship's company with superstition typical of ancient times drew lots in order to discover the culprit whose behavior might have angered the gods of the day. Of course, Jonah drew the short straw, figuratively speaking. As a matter of fact, he knew from the beginning that he was guilty and quite readily admitted that he had displeased his God. In a moment of repentant anguish he suggested he be thrown overboard so that the others might be saved. It was not a pleasant prospect, but Jonah was tossed over the side of the little ship. He hit the water with a generous splash, whereupon a large fish, commonly identified as a whale, swallowed the disobedient prophet.

It was some little distance to Nineveh, but the whale, with unerring navigational instinct, started thence with Jonah uncomfortably within. After three days and three nights, the prophet arrived at the port of Nineveh in his unconventional conveyance and was unceremoniously deposited on the shore. Jonah was not the least surprised. He was exactly where he knew he should be and where he should have gone in the first place. By way of his strange journey he had made the disconcerting discovery that he could not run away from the responsibility God had laid upon his mind and heart. It is a discovery most of us have yet to make.

I

We should not be too harsh in our judgment of Jonah, you and I. Of course, when God said, "Arise, go to Nineveh," Jonah should have gone at once. Nevertheless, Nineveh was not a pleasant place. The Ninevites were notoriously ungodly and nobody in his right mind would invite their scorn. Besides Jonah was not looking for trouble any more than the rest of us. He preferred to be as comfortable as possible. He was not interested in a bad situation he might improve, but rather wished a pious parish that would not strain either his temper or his courage.

Apparently, Jonah and God looked at life from opposite points of view. As God saw it, the best place in the world for a man of faith was the place that needed him to make it better. Jesus shared that same idea when he "set his face steadfastly to go to Jerusalem" to challenge the entrenched wrong of the Holy City of his fathers. Indeed, the saints of the earth who have breathed their benediction upon the human race unanimously have assumed they belonged where they were needed to make things better. Just call the roll, if you please, from Paul insisting that he must "see Rome also" to David Livingstone "painting the Dark Continent white" and you will find a company of great souls marching toward their Ninevehs believing they were needed there.

We Christians, however, are forever trying to dodge the fact we belong at Nineveh. During World War II when German cities were being bombed mercilessly from the air a Swedish commentator noted that in Germany thousands of men and women were simply dropping out of sight. Weary of the dull routine of their daily responsibilities they found it expedient to use the chaos caused by air bombardment as an easy way out. They could blame the bombs for loss of identity and let the world believe them dead. Here was an unparalleled opportunity to run out on unpleasant situations and onerous responsibilities. It was a chance to claim freedom. It was, however, a perilous freedom; a freedom to be lived in bondage to a bitter conscience and an unending sense of guilt. Bound for Tarshish, away from Nineveh, these weary souls plunged ahead toward tragic disillusionment.

You see, however we may wish it otherwise, we belong wherever things are wrong that we can make right, and there is no use trying to run away. If things are at sixes and sevens at home, that is our Nineveh. Home, then, is the best place in the world for us to be, to make it better, happier, more harmonious than it is. That is where we are needed most. Maybe the office is sheer bedlam, what with more work than can be done, half the staff inefficient, labor troubles and tempers on edge. There's no use running away or closing up shop. God needs you where you are to make rough waters smooth. Possibly your club has turned into a center of gossip which is spreading its infection right and left, far and wide. You are sick of it. As a Christian, however, the answer is not a letter of resignation. You belong where you are to improve the situation. Wherever there is conflict or confusion in business, in politics, in labor organizations, even in the church, that is where you belong. God is saying to you as He said to Jonah: "Arise, go to Nineveh." Those are your sealed orders.

Christianity never has been, never can be, a comfortable religion. The cross we honor in our worship is lovely and serene, a symbol of the noblest aspirations of our human kind; but once the cross was cruel and ugly; once it was smeared with the blood of one who dared to sail undaunted to Nineveh believing he belonged there. Today he calls with clarion voice: "Follow me. Follow me where sound the cries of race and clan; Follow me where things are wrong, where the world is out of joint, where life seems to be a tale told by an idiot. If you are my disciple, follow me."

II

Unhappily, we Christians do not follow him because we have other plans. We hear his call, "Follow me," but when the road leads toward Nineveh, we turn off toward Tarshish. Our difficulty lies in the character of the question we ask ourselves. When Jonah made his choice between destinations he asked himself: "What do I want from life?" It was a natural question and Jonah decided he wanted what Tarshish had to offer. The basic question, however, is not "What do I want?" As God sees the issue, the question we ought to put to ourselves is, "What is wanted of me?" Our little plans, based on the first question, are built upon the sand, tumbling all too easily into ruins. God's plans, built upon the second question, are founded upon solid rock.

Just see what happened to Jonah when he turned away from the question "What is wanted of me?" He knew the answer very well, it had been hammering upon the gates of his will for some time, "Arise, go to Nineveh." The prophet paints with grim realism the picture of what happened when he started for Tarshish. There was a storm which tossed Jonah's little boat upon the waves and frightened everybody. However, the storm was merely a symbol of what was happening inside Jonah. He was floundering in remorse, well-nigh swamped by a sense of guilt. Indeed, he was so depressed that he was quite willing to be thrown overboard to a watery grave. He even asked for the privilege of being thus disposed.

Jonah's experience is by no means strange. As a matter of fact, half the inward tensions that tear us apart are the consequence of our failure to do what we know is wanted of us. The psychological conflicts, which make our own souls the setting for civil wars, are produced by our own pursuit of personal preferences when God's plan points in the direction of Nineveh. Paul sensed the truth when he spoke so eloquently of the struggle between the flesh and the spirit, and Socrates gave utterance to the deepest experience of his own soul when Crito's urging would have set him free from prison and the peril of death. "I am inclined to think," he said, "that these muscles and bones of mine would have gone off long ago to Megara or Boetia—by the dog they would—if they had been moved by their own idea of what was best." But Socrates could not, would not play truant because a deeper logic than his own held him to his Nineveh. His peace of mind, his self-respect, his spiritual security all were contingent upon the choice he made.

Experience testifies to the fact that we defy the sealed orders of our souls at our own peril. Blindly following our own little plans, we invite inward storms and outward disaster. The truth is suggested by an experience related by Dr. Harry Emerson Fosdick whose father called back to the house one morning when he started to work: "Tell Harry to mow the lawn this morning if he feels like it. Tell him he had better feel like it." Harry might well have had other plans, perhaps a visit to a near-by pond where the fish would be biting, but the lawn had better be mowed. Tarshish always beckons when Nineveh calls but on the road to Tarshish there usually is a storm to rock the boat.

What is more, Nineveh inevitably becomes worse when we run off to Tarshish. The grass grows longer and more difficult to mow, the problem at home becomes more impossible, the confusion at the office grows more bewildering while we run elsewhere. No matter how far we run from our problems or how often we turn our backs on our difficulties we discover in the end they still are there waiting for us to meet them. Unhappily, the longer we put off the solution of our ills, the more difficult they become.

Our own little plans can wait; the inward imperatives of God cannot. So Jonah learned as he journeyed unhappily toward Nineveh inside the mythical whale. We cannot put off the question, "What is wanted of me?"

III

There was a final matter which troubled Jonah when his sealed orders were flung upon him: "Arise, go to Nineveh." He was convinced that he could do no good in the unholy city. He would be a minority of one in favor of righteousness and truth. God, however, was altogether certain that one prophet in Nineveh could alter the character of the place. Perhaps it would be more accurate to say that one man being used as an instrument of God could do something to change the people of Nineveh.

It is a vital issue now when we face the world and feel the extent of our futility. We seem quite sure that we are helpless to determine "the shape of things to come." Again and again we have halted in the presence of "impossible" situations saying to ourselves: "I might as well forget the whole business for all the good I can do." No doubt Jonah made out a good case for himself when he dodged Nineveh and started for Tarshish. He forgot one thing, however; he forgot that one man with God is a majority anywhere. Paul was only one man against the multitude, but he was a majority at Ephesus and Athens and even in Rome where he met his death. Augustine was one man against the tide that swept across the Roman Empire in the fifth century, but he was a majority of one, laying the foundation for a better future. William Wilberforce was one man against the slave trade, but, believe me, he was a majority of one. You see, when a man hurls himself into Nineveh to make the place better, he becomes a fellow toiler with God and in that moment links hands with the Eternal. He borrows the strength of God and leans upon the grace of God.

Just look at your own Nineveh and see what you and God can do there. It is a little short of amazing what one man with good will can do to untangle the strife and animosity inherent in the average community. When invective and bitterness come to his door, they stop there, transformed by calm counsel and a deep spirit into understanding. When criticism and gossip reach his ears, they stop there, to be changed into quiet helpfulness. Jesus called such folk "peace-makers," because they were nonconductors of the current of evil which, if allowed to go on gathering momentum, would, in the end, burst into flames.

Go one step further, and you will see why Nineveh has been made better than it was. It is because some lonely soul stood staunchly against the tide, to be a majority of one with God. Think, if you please, of any great movement which helped to make life different and always there was a man or woman standing alone for a while pointing the way, holding the torch, redeeming Nineveh. "He is worth much more than I can pay him," a man said to me not long ago of one of his employees. "Why?" I asked. "Well," he said, "five years ago when he came here we were having a terrible feud in the office. We were all at sword's points. Bill changed all that, somehow, and now we are pulling together even though the work is heavier than ever before."

Somewhere Dr. Paul Scherer describes a train wreck and a famous surgeon who had escaped injury standing beside a hurt passenger. He stood almost helplessly watching the man die. Then, turning to a bystander he said: "My God, if I just had my instruments." So God looks upon the Ninevehs around us to say: "All this could be changed if only I had my instruments." It is so, but we are his instruments, and we have run off, every man unto his own way. We do not see that Nineveh, no matter how dismal it appears, is an opportunity, not a dead end; a glorious challenge, not a grave. What is more, when we are God's instruments, we find the Living Christ at Nineveh more surely than anywhere else. He is there calling: "Follow me."

THE UPPER ROOM ON
MAIN STREET

<svg>※</svg>

Come unto me. . . .   MATTHEW 11:28
Go ye therefore. . . .   MATTHEW 28:19

<svg>※</svg>

IT IS A LITTLE SHORT OF AMAZING TO DISCOVER HOW DIFFERENTLY
individuals react to the Christian message. To one man it is a
source of comfort, peace and inward security; to another it is a
challenge to reform and social action. It has created its mystics and
its practical men of action. Both St. Simeon of Stylites, sitting atop
his pillar, and Cromwell, leading his armies, are the fruit of its
message. Indeed, the two types of response are suggested in the
words of Jesus. He says to his followers, "Come unto me," for rest
and peace. And then, lest men misunderstand, as they have done,
he went on with urgent passion, "Go ye therefore" into the market
place "where the race of men go by" to live out the faith that is in
you. He was both the mystic and the man of action. He calls us to
the Upper Room, but he wishes to be sure that the Upper Room is
hard by Main Street where life is lived in all its sordidness and
struggle.

"Come" and "Go" are two words which Jesus hurls upon his followers again and again as if he thought they summarized all life, as
indeed they do. As he saw it, life must be a combination of medita-

tion and motion, silence and struggle, prayer and push. The problem was, and is, to keep them in proper balance. We know that carbon monoxide taken into the lungs will kill, while carbon dioxide causes a headache. But carbon dioxide, in proper proportions, is a necessary element in the atmosphere. Life depends upon neither too much nor too little. Arsenic deals out either health or death depending upon the size of the dose. So, life that is all "Come," rest, meditation, silence, prayer, is sterile, while life that is all "Go," struggle, activity, drive, is devastatingly superficial.

Much of the agony and woe of our times is the consequence of too much "Go" and too little "Come." We are victims of motion without meditation and terrific drive without direction. It is reported that at the San Francisco Fair a few years ago one of the most popular entertainment gadgets was a machine designed to enable a man to kick himself. By leaning over and pulling a lever he could receive appropriate chastisement. The popularity of the kicking machine suggests how keenly we are aware that we need to be kicked for our stupidities. Of course, we note frequently by way of alibi that "hindsight is better than foresight," but the fact we realize we need to kick ourselves implies that our foresight should have been far better than it was. Our difficulty lies in the fact that we act without thinking, we push ahead without planning, we move without meditating first.

Long ago, in the days before automobiles, airplanes and streamlined trains enabled us to go nowhere faster than ever before, Elizabeth Fry, the Quaker ambassadress of God, was greatly troubled by the driving speed of the New World. She said she felt as if she were "all outside, no inside"; an apt description of all too many of us. It is not difficult to recognize that our generation is a victim of an unfortunate "degradation of the inner life." We have no wish to be alone with our thoughts; our thoughts are too insignificant to be interesting. We are fearful of quiet; its emptiness bores us. We prefer to go somewhere to do something—anything. Afterward, we feel like kicking ourselves.

Our inward sterility accounts for our amazing habit of getting up a head of steam when somebody coins an apt slogan. We will "Save the world for democracy" or for the "Four Freedoms" at a drop of the hat even though we have but small conception of either the meaning or the cost of democracy and less appreciation of the implications of the "Four Freedoms." Of course we are volatile, then, like high octane gasoline. We explode and then we are finished. We have no heart for the lonely, hot stretches, for the sweat and the tears that lie beyond the slogan and the initial victory. We are "all outside, no inside," all push, no prayer; all "Go ye therefore," no "Come unto me." But

> The Gods approve
> The depth, and not the tumult, of
> the soul.

We are too busy to create spiritually virile "insides." It is a curious matter, but we seem to have the feeling that it is a disgrace not to be, or seem to be, frightfully busy and perpetually under pressure. I can't seem to remember meeting anybody who admitted he had time on his hands. It would be poor taste to make any such admission, even for a minister! We would rather be busy and then afterward kick ourselves for making stupid mistakes, than to seek wisdom in quietness. We would rather plunge blindly after our slogans than soberly to think them through and judge them under God. That is our tragedy, and the world's.

Unhappily for us, most of the best things in life are not to be won by drive and speed and activity. "Go ye therefore" is an invitation to disaster unless we first have answered the call, "Come unto me." The pearls, worth all a man has, are not won by the latest neophyte in the "Go-Getters-Club." There is rather a quiet, silent beauty in the noblest things of earth which defies the plunging quest of human dynamos,

> I heard the booming sunset gun:
> I did not hear the sun go down.

Wisdom and judgment which obviate the need for kicking machines are born in quiet places. "Be still and know" is more than academic nonsense. We cannot really know in any other way. To be sure, we learn by experience, or do we? The incessantly active moth, flying into the camp lantern, singeing its wings and burning to death in the end, learns nothing from its tilts with the flame. What we learn through the pain of our burns is a consequence of our reflection. Hurt once, we reason then, that we may be hurt again. It is in the moment of meditation after experience that we learn or fail to learn the meaning of our hurt. Burned by fire, we learn quickly; but burned by our moral failures we digest the meaning of our experience with incredible reluctance. Why? Partly, at least, because we use furious activity as a means of stifling thought and massacring meditation. It hurts too much to think, so we run away madly. We learn nothing from our moral experience.

Nevertheless, it is only by way of honest meditation that we translate our hurts, our failures, our mistakes into growing points. When Henry Thoreau found his life one succession of disappointments and defeats after another, he understood the necessity for quietness. "I seek a garret," he said to Emerson, and then because his family invaded the garret sanctuary, he went to Walden Pond. He went, he said, "To find himself." He left for us the rich bequest of what he found, the mellowed wisdom and the sound judgment of stillness. No one today can read *Walden Pond* without gratitude for its gentle and homely wisdom; a wisdom distilled from the years of failure. "Be still, and know" was a text Thoreau understood profoundly.

Quite possibly our meditation will take us close to "the slough of despond" as it did Thoreau and Elijah too. Elijah almost thought too much after his devastating brush with Jezebel. He became the victim of an emotional storm that nearly destroyed his spirit. It seemed to him like an earthquake tinged with fire and brimstone; but when the storm was spent and quietness came, there was "the still small voice" speaking of calm and strength. Clearly, Elijah's emotional binge was a consequence of a toxic mind and a tired body. It was the climax of a furious effort to force an answer to a devastating problem that seemed to have no answer. "The still small voice" which came when the storm was spent suggests that problems are not solved by hard thinking alone. They are solved by surrender to the gentle voice that says, "Come unto me." "We grow into wisdom and judgment only when we are quiet enough to hear "the still small voice."

Happily, we are unable to manage God. He cannot be pushed or driven or coerced. "If the vision tarry" we had better "wait for it," or risk the peril of pushing on blindly without it. There is a popular advertisement which calls attention to "The pause that refreshes," a moment of cooling off with soda pop; but there is a wiser pause which refreshes with what Jesus called "living water." It comes when we give up trying to make things go our own way and come unto him who knows The Way. The dynamic Dante understood the meaning of the pause when he wrote what has been called the greatest line in all literature: "In His will is our peace." Such is the essence of all wisdom and judgment. It is distilled in the quietness when we come unto Him.

It should be noted, of course, that "our peace" is by no means static and outwardly untroubled. Dante found the "still small voice" abundantly disturbing, so troublesome, in fact, that when he followed its urging he was driven into exile. To answer the call, "Come unto me," is to be haunted by the piercing command, "Go ye therefore." Jesus calls us

> Up from the world of the many,
> To the over-world of the One,

but he promptly sends us

> Back to the world of the many,
> To fulfill the life of the One.

With one word he withdraws us from the world into the Upper Room of the spirit; with the next he hurls us back into the world,

> Where cross the crowded ways of life,
> Where sound the cries of race and clan.

The point is quite simple. He would direct our dynamic and motivate our activity on Main Street with the wisdom, the judgment and the faith of the Upper Room. Again and again we are reminded in the gospels that Jesus "went apart to pray," even to meditate and pray all night, but always on the morrow he was back in the market place toiling "in the power of the spirit." Meditation and prayer were not ends in themselves; they were a means of knowing and sources of power to do the will of God on the streets where men lived and labored.

Karl Barth quite rightly calls Christianity "a rest in battle." It is John Knox, praying at midnight so agonizingly and so long that his wife protested, only to be reproved for the interruption. He had won half of Scotland, he said, and if she had not interrupted, he would have won the other half. But John Knox did not leave the saving of Scotland to God. He toiled heroically, daring even to rebuke Bloody Mary for her sins at the risk of his life. His prayers were at once a source of rest and of resource. For him, and for us, Christianity is like a river blocked by a landslide, a river that brings unending reserves from the rear until with triumphant power it breaks the dam and moves on irresistibly. Its rest is only for the accumulation of reserves; its pause is for refreshment and renewal.

All this is of the utmost significance for us whose tired idealism and volatile irresolution are so obvious. Here is power to go on and on through the heat of the day and the weariness of the eventide. Here is something to relieve the feeling of being "all outside, no inside." Here is inward anchorage for our outward activity. Gladstone had this genius of alternation which took him from personal prayer to social power. "He lived," someone said, "from a great depth of being"; being in God, if you please. Dedication in the Upper Room wrought dynamic on the Main Streets of Britain.

Both power and direction flow from the Upper Room when we answer the call, "Come unto me." We are driven into the world then by a voice saying: "Go ye therefore." We are constrained by a spirit, crying:

> Rise up, O men of God!
> His kingdom tarries long.
> Bring in the day of brotherhood
> And end the night of wrong.

HELP THOU MINE UNBELIEF

❧

Lord, I believe; help thou mine unbelief.   MARK 9:24

⩗

T HE LAD WAS SICK, HIS FATHER SORE DISTRESSED. THEY HAD COME hopefully to the disciples, eager in their expectation of healing and help; but the disciples had failed miserably. Then came the Master to be greeted with fumbling words of faltering faith: "If thou art able to do anything take pity upon us and help us." The words, as Jesus said, were the words of an "unbelieving generation." But, they are our words in our distress; they express our feeling, too. We say our prayers and give utterance to our hopes in the shadow of a baffling doubt. Honestly, we expect very little of God. We have fallen into the habit of relying on ourselves, as if the issues of life were all in our own hands. Then, when we meet something we cannot manage we can muster only a cry, "If thou art able!"

But it is not enough, this doubtful word, "If you can." It takes more than that to make a man whole. "All things are possible for one who believes," but little can come of our doubt. Neither healing nor power is born of our mistrust. So Jesus affirmed as he looked with pity on father and son. The response was instant and anguished: "Lord, I believe, help thou mine unbelief." It was a human cry, echoing the mood of the multitudes; giving voice to the contradiction we feel within ourselves. It was faith speaking through the shadow of doubt and doubt pierced by the light of a saving faith.

39

There is a suggestion here that doubt is an aspect of faith which is quite normal. Your faith and mine sings hymns on a scale which reaches from sublime trust to troublesome uncertainty. Like Browning's bishop we are forever exchanging

> A life of doubt diversified by faith,
> For one of faith diversified by doubt.

Our faith is not often tranquil and steady. It ebbs and flows like the tides of the restless sea. Yesterday at dawn we awoke with a devout sense of thanksgiving and a certainty of the "goodness of God in the land of the living." Last night, after a trying, troublesome day we wondered somberly if God were only a mirage. Last week we lived adventurously on the sunny side of faith, but harsh blows fell upon us and the light failed, obscured by clouds of doubts. "If thou art able." We turn anxious eyes toward the heavens.

We need not be discouraged, however. Doubt is no stranger, even to the saints. Listen to the Psalmist: "I will say of the Lord, He is my refuge and my fortress: my God; in him will I trust." Here, surely, is one whose doubts are done. But no, there comes a lament on the heels of praise: "Jehovah, why hidest thou thy face from me?" There is Job, too. His lament is like unto ours: "Behold I go forward, but he is not there; and backward, but I cannot perceive him." Here doubt has nearly overwhelmed the spirit of the man. Nevertheless, the mood changes and slips into a shout of splendid trust: "Though he slay me, yet will I trust him."

Our quest for religious certainty, it seems, always is colored by uncertainty. Paul Laurence Dunbar puts his finger upon our experience when he says:

> Long time ago we two set out,
> My soul and I.
> I know not why,
> For all our way was tinged with doubt.

> I know not where
> We two may fare;
> Though still with every changing weather
> We wander, groping on together.[1]

So it is with us all. We grope and fumble in search of certainty, wishing we might escape the anxious question, "If thou art able." Haunted by our questionings we pray, "Lord, I believe, help thou mine unbelief."

The peril is that we shall cease groping on through our doubts and live only by our negations. Life's task, however, is to win faith strong enough to bear the burden of our doubts; faith vital enough to keep us going in spite of our doubts. No man ever drilled an oil well without being haunted by misgivings as the drill pressed downward toward producing structures. But only a fool would cease drilling halfway to the hoped-for pool. Doubts or no doubts he must go on. Says William Morris Hunt, the painter, "I tell you it is no joke to paint a portrait. . . . Into the painting of every picture that is worth anything, there comes a period of doubt and despair." Nevertheless, the genius of the painter lies in the will to push on through his doubt to creative achievement. The road to faith like the road to oil or to creative art is obstructed by devastating doubts, but no sane man gives up halfway to the end.

We do not need to solve all the mysteries of the universe before we acquire a faith to live by. The best that men ever have been able to do is to have faith enough to carry their doubts and go on through them; faith enough to go on drilling, not knowing what they will strike; faith enough to go on writing, or painting, or building a home in spite of their doubts; faith enough to go on following Christ even when the world defies God's dream. Robert Louis Stevenson sets the truth to the music of poetry in "the saddest and the bravest song he ever wrote":

[1] "Vagrants" from *The Complete Poems of Paul Laurence Dunbar.* Copyright, 1895–1913, by Dodd, Mead & Company, and used by permission.

God, if this were faith?
To go on forever and fail and go on again,
And be mauled to the earth and arise,
And contend for the shade of a word, and
    a thing not seen with the eyes,
With half of a broken hope for a pillow at night
That somehow the right is the right,
And the smooth shall bloom from the rough:
Lord, if that were enough?

Faith enough to carry our doubts! It is enough: perhaps it is all we can manage when "fears assail and doubts annoy." Maybe we can do no more than grope on through our uncertainties, following a man with a cross because somehow we cannot escape wishing his life were The Life, his way The Way. Inwardly we know the alternative is chaos and a vast lostness that leaves us impoverished, with our souls as dry as dust. So we dare not cease our groping on toward God, saying humbly, "Lord, I believe, help thou mine unbelief"; our faith barely able to bear the burden of our doubts. The glory of it is that there is growth in pushing on. No man ever was assailed more terribly by doubt than Martin Luther when the Peasants' Revolt devastated his parish. And yet, in toiling with his awful uncertainties, Luther achieved a faith which through the centuries has cast light along the pathway of the Protestant church. Out of his unending cry, "Help thou mine unbelief," there came a mighty affirmation, "I know him in whom I have believed." Doubts in the mind of Luther were the imps of Satan to be conquered by the love of Christ. They were not dead ends; they were thoroughfares to deeper truth and firmer faith. Doubt, you see, is an invitation to pilgrimage, a stimulus to spiritual discovery if we dare to push on through it.

There is a sense in which King Stanislaus of Poland was right when he insisted that "to believe with certainty we must begin with doubting," for the faith that is strong and sure is the faith that has not feared to ask questions; faith that has met doubt and overcome it. We are somewhat in the predicament of the small boy going swimming for the first time. He sees others floating quite comfortably on the water. But to plunge into deep water on the assumption that since others float, so can I, is to invite drowning. He had better begin with doubt concerning the friendliness of the deep. The deep is friendly only to those who have learned its secrets. It is wise to paddle and splash where it is shallow to get the feel of the thing. Doubt is dissipated by experience, even by the duckings which are implicit in the process of achieving faith in the water. What will you do with me if I trust myself to you? What must I do to be saved from sinking? Having learned the answers by way of experiment we plunge confidently into the deep, free and sure.

Confident belief in God and trust in His saving grace emerge similarly. Our doubts concerning the sustaining strength of God are not swept away by a single toss of the head. "He that willeth to do his will shall know," as Jesus said. Our doubts are dissipated only by doing His will, by learning the secret of His spirit so that we shall dare in the end to risk the deep waters. Perhaps the failure of the disciples to heal the wounded spirit of the lad whose father hoped so much from them was a consequence of their trying to swim in deep water before they had learned to trust its buoyant strength. In any event, in answer to their perplexed question, "Why could we not cast it out?" Jesus answered, "This kind can only be cast out by prayer."

You doubt that the grace of God can take your troubled, divided, futile life and make it whole? In God's name, don't stop with your doubt. It is only an invitation to spiritual discovery. You doubt that prayer can move mountains? Don't stop with your doubt, go on. Your doubt is a call to find reality beyond the simple glory of the hour of prayer. You doubt that forgiveness and love accomplish more than vengeance and hate in our world of Communist power?

Don't stop with your doubt, go on until you know. In simple ways, where the water is shallow, try out what Jesus says. You see,

> Our doubts are traitors
> And make us lose the good we oft might win
> By fearing to attempt.

Our doubts may be traitors, or they may be growing points. "Lord, I believe, help thou mine unbelief."

Happily, there will be times on your pilgrimage when you will "touch the stars with your fingertips," and for a while there will be no doubt in your heart. There will be moments when God is "nearer than breathing, closer than hands and feet." There will be no "if," then, but only a great affirmation, "Thou art able." Like Peter and James and John on the Mount of Transfiguration you will wish you might build tabernacles on the heights to keep the vision and preserve the faith so hardly won. But, as Jesus understood, tomorrow there will be the market place with its disillusionment, its greed, its embittering experiences. There will be home problems, business problems, mismanaged personal relationships, and the glorious vision, the splendid faith will falter and give way to "Lord, I believe, help thou mine unbelief."

Nevertheless, the secret of the life of power is to be found in the wisdom to live by the light of our finest hours of faith, not in the shadow of our darkest hours of doubt. If you are a fisherman you will remember days on the river when there seemed to be no fish anywhere in the vicinity. You would almost swear there were no fish in the river. But you will go fishing again! You will go because you cannot forget the day you filled your creel. As long as you fish that stream you will cast in the light of that wonderful day. Each morning when you step into the river to make your first cast you will be hoping today will be the day when the fish will bite again. Long ago you would have given up fishing if you lived by the light of the miserable day when you wondered whether there were any fish in the stream.

The point of the matter is that we are constrained of necessity to live by the light of our finest hours or we cannot really live at all. If there are times when integrity begets only a dishonest response, we have to live by the memory of honesty rewarded by grateful friendship. If there are days when kindness begets nothing but a tired back and a gruff rebuff, we have to keep on remembering the gratitude and love of another day. If there are hours when prayer seems to echo upon an empty void and we are sure that God is dead, we had better live by the glory of that other time when prayer was peace and God was very near. A man's doubts are his doom if he never pushes on beyond them, if he surrenders to their immobilizing devastation.

We must live by the light of faith which says, "Thou art able." We know, for once we called upon Thee, and we found the strength to see the shadows through; we called Thy name and peace was ours. Yea, even in the valley of the shadow, we "will fear no evil," for in one shining hour we found Thee. "Lord, we believe, help thou our unbelief."

Contemporary Tides

-->><<--

For it falls out
That what we have we prize not to the worth
Whiles we enjoy it, but being lack'd and lost,
Why, then we rack the value; then we find
The virtue that possession would not show us
While it was ours.
William Shakespeare, *Much Ado about Nothing*

OUR WEAPONS IN WORLD STRUGGLE

For the weapons of our warfare are not carnal, but mighty
through God to the pulling down of strongholds.

II CORINTHIANS 10:4

There is a tide in the affairs of men,
Which, taken at the flood, leads on to fortune;
Omitted, all the voyage of their life
Is bound in shallows and in miseries.

SUCH A TIDE IS UPON US NOW. AT HOME AND ABROAD THE OLD ORDER
is passing and we are feeling the birth pangs of the new, not yet
fully born. Traditions and venerable institutions are being challenged and as never before we are being constrained to "Give . . .
a reason for the faith that is in us." It may be that our generation
will set the pattern of political and spiritual life for a thousand
years to come.

The task before us is enough to stagger the imagination, for we
must take the tide, running now "at the flood" and turn it to creative purpose. Our engineers have learned by way of stern discipline
to use the floods that nature flings upon us to create power, systems
of irrigation and vast lakes. Working in obedience to nature, guided
by scientific principle, they have claimed the strength of flowing

49

tides. There is at least a chance that we may seize the tide of our time and use it to create the better world of which we dream. There is a chance if we are guided by the mind of Christ. "Whosoever heareth these sayings of mine, and doeth them, I will liken him unto a wise man, which built his house upon a rock" whose stability time and tide cannot destroy.

I

Once long ago when an old order was being shaken, and new forces were stirring in and around the Roman Empire, Paul faced his task as a Christian. How could he claim the flowing tide and use it in the name of Jesus Christ? What could he do to shape the course of things? One thing was clear to him as he spoke to his contemporaries. "The weapons of our warfare are not carnal," he wrote, "but mighty through God to the pulling down of strong holds." He had a curious notion, fortified by his faith in Christ, that "the shape of things to come" is determined "not by might nor by power," but by the "spirit."

Paul knew enough of violence and coercion to realize their victories were altogether shallow. Violent death had not put an end to the power of his Lord. Imprisonment, stoning, beatings with the cat-o'-nine-tails had turned out, as he saw it, "unto the progress of the gospel." He had an absurd, ridiculous confidence that even the might and overwhelming power of the Roman Empire could not conquer the little church he was building in the Master's name. There was a spirit, "mighty through God," that was more than a match for Rome. Rome's might stood on "feet of clay" that could not bear the weight of civilization when storms blew in from the deeps of human restlessness. Paul was certain that the future belonged to the ideas and ideals, the faith and the fellowship that flowed from the mind of Christ.

The weapons of our warfare are moral, spiritual and intellectual, and they are far mightier than we suspect. In obedience to Christ, they dig to the roots of problems and issues, and we have to begin with roots. If the carburetor of your automobile is not properly adjusted, you do not cure the miss in the motor by changing the spark plugs. If you have rheumatism in your joints, you do not cure the trouble with liniment. You have to find the source of poison and infection elsewhere in your body. When the world is torn by angry conflict the way it is, we cannot cure its ill with atomic mustard plasters. We have to get at the root of the trouble. The "weapons of our warfare" deal with roots.

Unhappily, we have a habit of trying to cure deep-seated ills with surface applications. Even casual observance of the American scene suggests how much we need to "launch out into the deep." Our smart advertisers have made fortunes appealing to minds "bound in shallows." You would think, to hear the advertisers, that a television set in your home would give your children all the benefits of a college education quite painlessly. Commentators suggest that the world will be saved without further ado if we build an air force capable of pulverizing Russia. Military leaders tell us a few atomic bombs strategically dropped as a preventive measure now will settle everything. "Bound in shallows" the way we are, the only weapons we can think of are carnal.

Our superficial thinking has turned life into farce or comedy, when as de Unamuno, the Spanish philosopher, says, it is tragedy. By that he means that life makes sense and we reap what we sow. A farce is a play in which the plot hinges on accidents. If a man falls into a swimming pool with his clothes on or blunders into the wrong apartment by mistake, the event may be very funny, but it does not follow from any moral failure of the man. Tragedy, however, is very different. It is a play in which effect follows cause and things happen for obvious reasons. Hamlet, Macbeth and King Lear met disaster because progressive deterioration of character in each of them made death inevitable. Our contemporary crisis is in the nature of tragedy, and to blame Korea and the cold war on Stalin and the Communists alone is to turn tragedy into burlesque and to miss the fact that the moral sickness of civilization made both of them.

If there is logic in life, as any thoughtful person can see there is, then our illness has gone beyond the help of secular expedients. Nothing less than a moral revolution, striking at the heart of our sickness, can save us. We may tinker all we please with economic systems, international associations and social security programs, but we shall get nowhere until we experience a moral reformation reaching into every area of our national life and touching the springs of private thinking. It is a reformation that must start with us, for the moral greatness of a nation and the wisdom of its leaders depend upon the greatness of its people.

A recent writer on political theory dropped into the middle of his erudite discourse this true and homely statement: "A man should not say: 'I live in a democracy,' but rather, 'I experienced democracy last Tuesday afternoon.'" How do we experience democracy on a snowy Tuesday afternoon? I experienced democracy once when I met a man voluntarily and honestly seeking a solution to a difficult civic problem. Nobody demands it of him, but he is so fine that he demands it of himself. I experienced democracy when I visited with a labor leader, honestly considering the problems of labor and industry with fair-minded courage.

The "weapons of our warfare" inevitably fling us back upon ourselves and find the key to the sickness of society in the darkness of our souls. They rest our hope on our integrity, our faith, our greatness of spirit, and lead us inescapably to the conclusion of Gladstone, seventy odd years ago: "I am convinced," he wrote, "that the welfare of mankind does not depend upon the state or work of politics. The real battle is being fought in the world of thought, wherein men decide for or against belief in God and the gospel of Christ." The future hangs on how we decide. Shall we embrace the mind of Christ or blunder on toward new disaster? Basically, "The weapons of our warfare are not carnal."

II

Paul faced the sickness of the Roman world with insight borrowed from the mind of Christ. He sensed the futility of coercion and of meeting evil with evil, but he had a secret weapon which he made quite public. "Be not overcome by evil," he wrote, "but overcome evil with good." It was a novel notion for a world accustomed to "an eye for an eye and a tooth for a tooth." But Paul was altogether certain that his secret weapon was "mighty through God to the pulling down of strongholds." He was sure because he had tested the truth in the fires of conflict and suffering.

Our mood, however, is largely alien to the mind of Christ. In the thirties a distinguished senator suggested we would be wise to spend a few millions of dollars building hospitals and colleges in Japan to cultivate the good will of the Japanese people. That, he remarked, would be better insurance against war with Japan than billions spent on armament. His suggestion was greeted with contempt as altogether too sentimental to be considered. Nevertheless, as General MacArthur noted, Communism has become identified as the benefactor of the common man. He added that the most decisive evidence the West can offer in rebuttal is to be found in the medical missions of the Christian church. All over Asia today are men and women who know from firsthand experience that Christianity cares. They are a mighty bulwark against the tide that threatens them and us. In Africa, where Communism is striking now, Albert Schweitzer and the thousands who have known his healing ministry are a mighty source of strength to stem the tide. What is more, thousands of young men and women educated in the Christian colleges of China and Korea, India and Pakistan are living evidence of Christian concern for ordinary people. Believe me, they are a significant factor in the world struggle of today.

No doubt there have been failures in the administration of Marshall Plan aid for the nations of Europe, but there can be no question of the fact that on a national scale we have given decisive evidence of the fact that it is possible to "overcome evil with good." It is more than probable that all of Europe would have been in the Communist camp had it not been for the generosity of this nation. My one regret is that we have undercut the impact of our generosity with a negative motive. Instead of affirming our concern for human values and testifying to our faith in the brotherhood of man under the Fatherhood of God, we have merely affirmed our will to "contain Communism." Our announced motive undercut the moral power of our generosity.

What bothers me now is that the cold war has totally and completely lost its spiritual front. That loss of spiritual front was strikingly illustrated during the 1952 presidential election, when both major political parties pressed their claims to voter support in terms of their opposition to Communism. By and large the best Communist haters were the best vote-getters and vice versa. Nobody seemed to have any idea of overcoming evil with good anywhere along the line. The trouble is that merely hating Communists does not solve any problems. Ralph Waldo Emerson put his finger on our predicament once after he had written a lecture full of pretty pictures of Utopia. He ruefully noted, "I found when I had finished my new lecture that it was a very good house, only the architect had unfortunately omitted the stairs." That is the trouble with merely hating Communists. It omits the stairs to a better world.

Once during the Civil War when the policies of the North were in flux, Secretary Seward was trying to fashion some basic positive principles of action. He was troubled by the people who did most of their thinking with their emotions. He told the story of an Irish soldier who rushed into his captain's tent, gun in hand, shouting: "What shall I fire at, Captain? I don't see nobody." The Captain smiled: "Fire at the crisis. Don't you know there is a crisis in this country?" The simple fact is that too many people are firing at the crisis and too few people are putting stairs in the house.

When Paul wrote that the "weapons of our warfare" are "mighty to the pulling down of strongholds," he was thinking of positive weapons, not negative ones. "Overcome evil with good," he wrote with the sure knowledge that only the positive practice of the Christian ethic in both personal and national affairs can save us.

III

That leads me to Paul's basic point. Dr. Moffatt translates the words with eloquent power: "I take every project prisoner to make it obey Christ." That was his mission in life. Every sermon he preached, every letter he wrote, every journey he made was infused with his high purpose. He lived and worked in the sober faith that projects rooted in Christian principle could not fail. They would be "mighty through God to the pulling down of the strongholds" of opposition. As he put it, "Whatsoever is born of God overcometh the world."

Historians have noted again and again that World War I ended months, if not years before it might have ended because the moral grandeur and power of Woodrow Wilson's Fourteen Points undermined the German will to resist. But the peace that followed the war was not built on principles. We had professed allegiance to principles, fourteen of them: and our enemies, trusting in our allegiance to those principles, laid down their arms. Then, as Herbert Hoover has so clearly described, we cynically tore up nine of those principles and made a peace by way of horse-trades among the victorious Allies. By such a peace was begotten inevitably World War II. Practical people have no time for principles! Unfortunately, practical people find their strongholds pulled down by the principles they reject.

Unless we take policies and plans prisoner "and make them obey Christ," we are undone. We cannot be, as Sumner Welles says we have been, "consistently inconsistent," with policies of expediency and expect to win the world struggle in which we are engaged. We cannot barter the rights of the Poles in Poland and the Chinese in Manchuria as we did at Yalta and Potsdam and then expect the world to believe in our integrity. We cannot barter the rights of Arabs in Palestine on the altar of domestic politics and then expect the world to trust our principles. Either we will make our policies "obey Christ," or we will forfeit our right to win the world struggle.

Our difficulty now is that we cannot escape history. Yesterday will not let us go. When Neville Chamberlain came back to London after a visit with Hitler in which he had sacrificed and betrayed Czechoslovakia, he announced that he had won "Peace for our time." Peace, however, never is won by abandoning principles, as he soon discovered. Today's perfidy is tomorrow's disaster. One by one we make expedient choices, and each expedient choice leads to another until there is no way out. The unnecessary choices of yesterday lead us inexorably to the necessity for violent conflict today.

There still is time, but it is later than we think. There still is time to capture the issues of the present and make them prisoners "to obey Christ." There still is time for an eloquent and stirring affirmation of the principles for which we stand, and a courageous policy dedicated to the principles. There still is time to win the struggle for the minds of men if we do not squander all of our resources on military mustard plasters that will not finally cure our ills. "The weapons of our warfare are not carnal, but mighty through God to the pulling down of strong holds."

RESTORE THE RAMPARTS

And thou shalt be called, The repairer of the breach, The restorer of paths to dwell in.   ISAIAH 58:12

FORTY YEARS OF EXILE IN BABYLON HAD LEFT MOST OF THE HEBREW people morally and spiritually exhausted, and yet a remnant remained vitally and vigorously alive. When Cyrus set them free they returned to the ruined city of Jerusalem with joy. They were full of dreams and plans and even the rubble of a once proud city did not discourage them. They went at the task of rebuilding with enthusiasm. But the difficulties were great, and as they struggled amidst ruin month after month their enthusiasm ran off with their sweat. The task was greater than they had dreamed. There were times when they wished for their slavery. It had cost them less in blood, sweat, tears and toil.

Isaiah felt the mood of his people and he responded to it with tenderness and compassion. He saw the walls of the city, still breached in a dozen places where siege engines had battered them down forty years before. The temple, once the pride of Zion, remained a mess of timber and stone, piled in a shapeless heap. Here and there order was coming out of the chaos, but so little had been done, and so much remained to be done. The prophet felt the burden of his task. Someone, however inadequate must revive the people and renew their faith in their dream. So Isaiah painted a picture of what could be, a panorama of the Holy City renewed in all its glory. He pictured the generations of the future looking back, and then he said, "Thou shalt be called, The repairer of the breach, The restorer of paths to dwell in."

I

The prophet had no illusions. He did not minimize the task before his contemporaries. It was beyond their powers without God. He made that clear. They never would be able to carry on without a faith to keep them on their feet when they were faltering. They never would rebuild the shattered walls for the defense of their beloved city without courage beyond anything they could muster on their own. Either they would have to begin with God or they would end with failure. But if their faith was adequate for their task, "Thou shalt be called, The repairer of the breach, The restorer of paths to dwell in."

There is a striking kinship between us and the Jews of Isaiah's day. The proud and triumphant civilization of Christendom has been battered almost beyond recognition in our time. The walls defending the noblest and best in our heritage have been breached in a hundred places by depression and war and cold war. When we consider our world we wonder if its rebuilding is beyond us. The problems of our time defy our human intelligence. Like the Jews of old, trying to rebuild Jerusalem, we are beset by enemies determined to thwart the rebuilding. Our enemies, like those of the Jews, have everything to gain by obstruction. If the walls are soundly rebuilt, they are finished.

When we consider the breaches we are trying to repair, we are staggered by the task. There is the economic breach. The Western world, having exhausted itself in war, is staggering on the brink of bankruptcy. The old channels of trade which provided the economic sinews of national life have been disrupted by the Iron Curtain.

The need for military defense against the threat from the East has delayed the normal processes of recovery. Ancient fears and the legacy of neighborhood quarrels have thwarted a unified effort to repair the economic breach. We have tried to repair the breach, pouring billions into Europe to restore confidence and hope. No nation ever tried so desperately to rebuild the economic foundations of Christendom. Generations yet to be may well call us "the repairer of the breach, the restorer of paths to dwell in."

The economic breach in Christendom's wall of defense is serious enough, but the political breach is equally dangerous. We sensed the danger when we brought the nations together under the banner of the United Nations. When atomic bombs burst with shattering effect over Nagasaki and Hiroshima it was as if the voice of God had thundered above the mushroom cloud, "Now will you believe you must have one world or none?" Even the scientists are frightened by the possibilities of atomic warfare, and some of them are asking anxiously, "Shall we go on?" We cannot afford the luxury of two worlds, and yet the political division between the slave and the free is a relentless fact of our time. We are baffled when we ask, "How shall we repair the breach, and restore paths for men to dwell in securely?"

The economic breach and the political breach are altogether apparent as we consider our time, but no less real is the moral breach. We see it in our national political life. Someone remarked not long ago that the most disturbing fact about our time is "the loss of the sense of shame." We defend wrong in the name of expediency and we justify the worst in the name of necessity. We take corruption for granted. Surveys before the 1952 presidential election revealed that "corruption in government" was a minor issue in the campaign because of the common assumption that politics as such is corrupt. A few years ago we would not have believed it possible that men would insist lying is right. We were not so good that we never lied and pretended to be telling the truth, but we never took the position that lying was a virtue. But in our time propaganda assumes the right to lie and extols the virtue of telling the same lie until it is believed. Under the threat of outside danger, we are quite willing to dispense with the truth and justify our behavior as a national virtue. It is high time we seriously undertook the business of repairing the moral breach in our civilization, and restoring paths of integrity for men to dwell in.

II

It is quite unnecessary to belabor the fact that the walls defending our civilization have been breached on the economic, the political and the moral fronts. What is not so clear is that the obvious breaks in the wall are consequences rather than causes. Long before the Babylonians fell upon Jerusalem, Isaiah sensed the weakness that would make the walls vulnerable. The weakness was in the men who dwelt within the walls. "Bring no more vain oblations," he shouted in the name of God, as if the people had turned their religion into a sham without the substance of devotion to the highest. As he saw it, the real problem was a deficit of personal devotion to the God of Abraham and Isaac and Jacob. If those inside the walls lacked devotion to something sublimely vital they might as well leave the walls in their state of ruin.

In our time there is very little point in trying to rebuild the economic, political and even the moral walls unless there is in us a great devotion to something really worth defending. The story of the Great Wall of China is worth remembering. Built to defend the country against foreign aggression, it stretches for fifteen hundred miles along the northern provinces of the nation. It is a colossal structure, fifteen to twenty-five feet thick at its base and rising in height from twenty to thirty feet. But the Great Wall of China never stopped an invader. Even in the days before the advent of modern weapons it never halted a serious invasion, even though it constituted a formidable barrier to the progress of an army. The reason for the failure of the Great Wall was very simple. Somebody inside the wall always opened a gate somewhere to let the invader through. Somebody inside the wall always could be bought for a price. So, the wall was breached from the inside, not from the outside.

We can rebuild the economic, political and even the moral walls with which to defend our civilization, but in the end we will get nowhere without a great devotion to the values and the ideals of the Kingdom of God which undergird our common life and make the walls worth rebuilding and defending. If there is a deficit of devotion inside the walls, building the walls is a sheer waste of effort and we spend our toil and treasure in vain. The simple truth is that we cannot defend anything worth defending without selfless devotion to the highest we know.

In recent years, for example, we have been trying to defend sports against the invasion of gamblers and racketeers, and against commercialism. The attacks on the integrity of sports from the outside have been relentless. Well-meaning alumni have offered football stars anything from automobiles to a monthly salary under the table for entering one university or another. Basketball stars have been offered bribes to throw games or shade points. So, in order to defend the integrity of athletics, college authorities have written codes and even employed detectives to uncover infractions of the rules. But rules and threats and detectives cannot thwart the invasion of dishonesty into sports, not if there is a deficit of devotion to good sportsmanship in the men who man the walls of collegiate sports.

We have been worried, too, about the security of our "free enterprise system." So, we are trying to build walls to stop the infiltration of communist and socialist ideas. We scan high school and college textbooks to remove passages which we regard as dangerous. We threaten and denounce teachers who seem to us to be too liberal. But we are starting from the wrong end. The problem is to inspire a great devotion to the spiritual ideals and the moral values that undergird our system. The most serious threat to our system abides in the fact that in our common life and in our educational system we are unconsciously cultivating a deficit of devotion. In most American colleges and universities, for example, material success is the predominant goal of the educational process. A young man at Ohio State University was quoted by *Life* in the March 28, 1949, issue as follows:

We're shooting to be tagged by the General Motors or General Electric or some outfit like that before we graduate. That's why you've got to figure all your plays from the time you're a sophomore—the right courses with grades that are good but not too good, . . . plenty of campus activity to show leadership, . . . and some athletics so that the personnel jokers from the big companies who look over the records will know that you are no swish.

Unfortunately, education dedicated to nothing more significant than financial success is infinitely more dangerous to the American system than any communist teacher anywhere.

When we live in a vacuum of devotion to the highest we open the gates to the lowest. If we cultivate in our children a deficit of devotion to the highest by making material values the goal of living we invite the destruction of our way of life from the inside. We inspire the belief that integrity is less important than success and honor far less significant than a well-padded bank account. In due time we get precisely what we have—corruption in public life, dishonesty in private life, gamblers and racketeers and a loss of a sense of shame about the whole business.

It is the weaknesses inside the wall, eating at the heart of our common life, that constitute our major peril in a time of rebuilding. Nothing can save us in the end but a renewal of devotion to Jesus Christ as lord of life. We cannot defend our civilization against the tides that threaten if we suffer from a deficit of devotion, and we cannot renew our devotion without the church of Jesus Christ. It is the one institution in our times whose business it is to inspire devotion to the noblest in our human heritage. It is the one voice pleading for loyalty to the living God in whose hands are the issues of life and death.

III

It is not only a deficit of personal devotion inside the walls that threatens our Western civilization in this time of rebuilding. There is also a second weakness within which may be described as a misdirection of devotion. Isaiah felt it in his time. It was apparent in the days before the Babylonians overwhelmed the nation and sacked the Holy City. The nation had usurped the place of God. Treaties and alliances were to be kept only if they seemed to benefit the nation. Honor and justice had departed from the Hebrew vocabulary, and the security of Judah was the final arbiter of the right. It is significant to note that the destruction of the nation was exactly coincident with the misdirection of its devotion.

The same misdirection of devotion in our time is opening the gates from within for those who would destroy our civilization and our way of life. Commonly we say, "My country, may she ever be right; but right or wrong, my country." It sounds patriotic when we put it that way, but in reality it is the patriotism of the blind. Put another way, the truth is plain. There are multitudes of men who are saying: "My party, may she ever be right; but right or wrong, my party." Not so long ago a man told me he had voted for Democratic candidates for political office for forty years and he intended to vote Democratic again. It occurred to me that the Republicans must have been right at least once in forty years! Men are saying, "My union, may she ever be right, but right or wrong, my union." So they blindly follow their leaders regardless of the cost to the nation.

The trouble in each case is that the country, the party or the union claims the devotion that belongs to God. What the country, the party or the union wants becomes the final arbiter of right and wrong, and the consequences are serious beyond calculation. There is a striking and disturbing illustration of the tragedy of misdirected devotion in Herbert Hoover's story of the great depression. On the domestic front there is a grim recital of obstruction and cantankerousness thwarting recovery for political advantage. There is a terrible recital of stubbornness and selfishness on the part of nations, each scrambling to gain economic advantage at the expense of the other. Mr. Hoover sums up the tragedy in a single sentence when he says of Pierre Laval of France: "He had a passionate devotion to France." But that devotion to France broke the bank of Austria, drove England off the gold standard and through the tragedy of inflation in Germany gave rise to Hitler. So, says Mr. Hoover in substance, devotion to either a party or a nation at the expense of greater values is social suicide.

Let there be no mistake, disunity inspired by misdirected devotion invites the inner decay of all that is best in our heritage. Our forefathers were well aware of the peril when they pledged their "lives," their "fortunes" and their "sacred honor" to a new concept of freedom for mankind. It cost many of them their lives and their fortunes while they struggled from Lexington and Concord to Valley Forge. But notice, if you will, that they did not worship their country. Indeed, they had no country. They were thirteen states and they spent half their time quarreling with one another and the other half fighting the British. They were a tenuous collection of men and women of mixed motives who were wedded together finally by their great devotion to something they called "freedom." It was not something they invented. They insisted they were "endowed" with it by their "creator." They gave their devotion to a great idea, to the sacredness of individual life and conscience under God. As a consequence freedom was fashioned into the flesh of a nation, into its Constitution and Bill of Rights. The word "freedom" was clothed with the fabric of a system of government so that the nation itself became for all the world the symbol of a dynamic idea. Our country became in truth "the land of the free and the home of the brave."

In our time, however, something disturbing is happening. We are suffering from a misdirection of devotion. We are shifting the emphasis from the idea of freedom under God to the instrument we fashioned to preserve it, and we seem to be trying to preserve the instrument without the idea. Little by little we are turning the nation into an end in itself and forgetting that the nation is only the means by which the possibilities of a thrilling idea can be fulfilled. We are worshiping the instrument at the expense of the idea and as a consequence we are destroying what we meant to preserve.

Some day perhaps we will understand what Jesus meant when he said: "Seek ye first the kingdom of God and his righteousness." Freedom is one essence of that kingdom, and no other devotion is big enough to preserve our freedom. No other devotion can preserve the integrity of the walls within while we build ramparts for our defense. God stands in judgment upon our nation, our parties, our unions, and nothing but devotion to the Kingdom of God can save us.

IV

Unless the church can revive our devotion to the Kingdom of God the stoutest walls we build, economic, political, moral, cannot save our civilization. Rabbi Louis Binstock notes that the one unfailing bulwark of civilization in Germany under Hitler was the church. He describes the power and daring of its great devotion to the Kingdom of God as he saw it with his own eyes. He was worshiping with Christian people because the synagogues were closed. The church was filled to capacity, with men and women pouring over the steps and crowding the aisles, hungering for the simple words of the Lord uttered by their pastor, Martin Niemoeller. He heard Martin Niemoeller just four days before he was imprisoned and, he says, "only a man religiously inspired and unalterably determined to render unto God that which belongs to God no matter at what cost, could have dared so openly to defy Hitler." A Nazi degree just had been issued banning contributions to the Confessional Synod of Germany, yet Niemoeller called for an offering. Suddenly, a band of Hitler youths rushed in, clubbing the keepers of the collection boxes shouting, "It is forbidden."

Niemoeller merely raised a hand and announced a hymn. And above the sounds of the coins jingling into the boxes and the frenzied bellowing of the enraged Nazis could be heard the swell of that majestic song:

> A mighty Fortress is our God,
> A Bulwark never failing;
> . . . .
> For still our ancient foe
> Doth seek to work us woe;
> . . . .
> And though this world, with devils filled,
> Should threaten to undo us;
> We will not fear, for God hath willed
> His truth to triumph through us.

Say what you will, devotion such as that is the only security we have against the ravages of evil, the only power there is to preserve our unity in one world, our freedom and our integrity. Thank God for the church in a day like this. It is the root of devotion that will enable us to be repairers of the breach, and restorers of paths to dwell in.

WANTED—RESPONSIBLE
CITIZENSHIP

❦

"And he said unto me, Son of man, stand upon thy
feet."   EZEKIEL 2:1

P LATO, WHO LIVED AT THE CLOSE OF THE GOLDEN AGE OF DEMOCRACY
in Greece, watched the crumbling of the democratic order with
mixed feelings. His faith in democracy had been shattered when the
Athenians put Socrates to death. He never forgave democracy for
the judicial murder of his beloved teacher. The experience of Greece
led Plato to the conclusion that democracy always and inevitably is
corrupted by human greed and pride. The reason, as he saw it, is
simple: Democracy gives the individual more freedom than he can
manage. Plato, therefore, advocated rule by an aristocracy of intelligence, wherein philosophers are kings and kings philosophers.
In a sense, Plato fathered the political "brain trust."

If it is true, as Plato contends, that democracy gives the individual more freedom than he can manage, then it follows that democracy is doomed ultimately to self-destruction. If we start with
Plato's premise, we arrive inevitably at Plato's conclusion. The decisive question concerns the premise: are we indeed incapable of
managing our freedom? It is significant to notice that in the golden
age of Athenian democracy, Pericles observed: "We are restrained

67

from lawlessness chiefly through reverent fear." But by the time of Plato, the Greek gods had been so largely discredited, that the restraint of "reverent fear" no longer held pride and greed in check. Without the restraint of "reverent fear" democracy gave the Greeks more freedom than they could manage.

I

The implication of Plato's thinking is that his only alternative to rule by absolute power is allegiance to an absolute ideal that is grounded in God. Freedom is possible only where men are morally disciplined by reverent devotion to Jesus Christ as Lord. Abraham Lincoln felt the truth when he prefaced his promise of "a new birth of freedom" after the Civil War with the words "Under God." He understood that freedom demands spiritual and moral discipline. Without reverent allegiance to the moral will of God revealed in Jesus Christ, democracy gives the individual more freedom than he can manage.

The question before our times is whether we have enough reverence to save us from ruin. It is a moot question. Huey Long remarked shortly before he was shot after a Sunday night session of the Louisiana legislature: "I can buy legislators like sacks of potatoes." What is more, the moral climate of political life does not seem to have changed greatly, when we note the present league between crime and politics and the use of the so-called "pork barrel" to influence votes in Congress. Without reverence for a God who demands inward integrity all is permitted that is personally or politically profitable.

Freedom demands devotion to an ideal which rises above the conflicting interests of individuals. It requires a "categorical imperative," as Immanuel Kant called it, for unless you and I acknowledge the authority of an ideal, we have no basis for mutual trust in each other, as we are discovering in our dealings with Soviet Russia. The truth is suggested on the baseball diamond. I recall listening once to a baseball game eloquently reported by a radio commentator. It was one of those games in which the umpire seemed to be in hot water most of the time. The White Sox and the Athletics were fighting for the glory of their respective cities. There was a near riot when the umpire called a runner safe at home plate. There was a furious debate over whether a hard-hit ball into right field was a home run or a two-base hit. The umpire and the hitters could not seem to agree on balls and strikes, and the fans vigorously indulged their right to boo. Everybody had a good time except the umpires.

What interested me, however, was the fact that all the arguments centered around questions of fact or judgment. There was no argument about the rule that a runner is out if he is tagged off base. There was no argument over the rule that a pitched ball is a strike if it comes over any part of the plate between the shoulders and the knees of the batter. The arguments and the debates concerned the judgment of the umpires who had to decide whether a runner was on or off base when he was tagged and to determine whether a pitched ball was or was not over the plate in the proper area. Both the players and the umpires acknowledged their allegiance to an ideal, categorical standard of judgment. Without that mutual allegiance baseball could not be played. It is the common acceptance of mutually agreed standards that undergirds the game.

What is true for baseball is true for life. If standards of right and wrong become matters to be decided on the basis of expedience nobody can trust anybody. If balls and strikes are decided merely by the whim of the umpire or the secular state with no allegiance to an ideal beyond, the game becomes a brawl in which the right of the strongest becomes final. If the businessman on Main Street cannot depend upon the state, his competitors, his customers and his sources of supply, to be loyal to an ideal standard of integrity, he cannot do business. He can cope with an occasional cheater, but he cannot cope with moral chaos, wherein the rules are changed to suit the demands of a "party line."

To be sure, there are times when absolute standards are difficult to apply. Strikes seldom come over the middle of the plate. They barely catch or miss the corners and there is room for differences of opinion when the umpire announces his decision. Similarly it is often difficult to make moral choices because the issues are not clear cut. There usually is a little bit of bad in the best alternative and a little bit of good in the worse. Nevertheless, we are lost without reverence for something that lifts our choice above mere self-interest. If we cannot achieve the absolute, at least we can approximate it.

It is here in the realm of difficult decisions that the Christian ethic of love finds its relevance. "Love seeketh not its own." It transcends rules and regulations, tempering justice with love. It goes beyond the legal requirements of integrity. Called safe at the plate in a rugged slide, the Christian refuses to be safe if he knows he was tagged before he touched the bag. He is more interested in giving justice than in getting it. His integrity is constrained by reverence for God in whom he "lives and moves and has his being." He is a dependable customer and a sound risk at any bank. His word is better than his bond. He is the foundation upon which a free society can be built. His freedom is manageable because it is under the constraint of his reverence.

Democracy gives the individual more freedom than he can manage, however, unless he is inwardly constrained by a vital allegiance to God, revealed in Jesus Christ. The future, therefore, hinges upon whether or not we are able to produce a generation of young men and women whose reverence will undergird their freedom. We have been living for some time now on our spiritual capital, spending beyond our income. Either we will replenish our spiritual capital as responsible citizens concerned for the future, or we shall leave our children with resources inadequate to sustain their freedom.

Freedom is an invitation to disaster unless it is sternly disciplined by reverence. There can be no freedom except freedom "under God."

II

It should be noted, too, that democracy gives the individual more freedom than he can manage unless he is reverently aware of his responsibility for the creative use of his God-given talents. "Under God" he is a co-worker with God in all creative toil. "I must work the works of him that sent me," said Jesus. So must we all. That conviction is basic to a democratic society. The carpenter, the bricklayer, the attorney and the engineer, indeed "every toiler in the quarry," belongs to the "regiment of God." Creative toil is a spiritual oblation. Like the rower in his shell awaiting the race, democratic society assumes that "every man must pull his own weight and a little bit more." That is his spiritual responsibility as a child of God.

The contemporary revolt against individual responsibility suggests that we have lost confidence in the spiritual meaning of our toil. The significance of work has been sacrificed on the secular altars of wages, hours and profits. The fact that we are creative co-workers with God, born to share in the labor of creation, has been obscured by the primacy of the profit motive. Inevitably, therefore, we have become less and less concerned about productive contribution, and more and more interested in extravagant reward. The hitchhiker thumbing a ride has become a symbol of our psychological mood. We want to be coddled and pampered and carried along as if the world owed us a living. For a while a paternalistic government assumed the role of Dodo in *Alice in Wonderland,* saying pontifically: "Everybody has won and all must have prizes." Our forefathers assumed that prizes were the rewards for material or intellectual production. We decided there should be prizes for everybody, whether or not they tried to participate in the contest.

There are in every society those who have no wish to stand on their own feet as responsible citizens and creative co-workers with God, if they can persuade a benevolent government to give them a prize of one sort or another. The contest for prizes has become a great American game popularly known as "Subsidy." I recall the days when I was trying to teach my three boys to play baseball. The two older boys agreed that their small brother ought to have a subsidy, a handicap. So, when we played ball, he got four strikes instead of three. That one strike subsidy remained in effect for some months, until it assumed the proportions of a vested right. Even when the little brother got to the point of hitting the ball all over the lot, he still assumed he ought to have four strikes. There came a day, however, when his older brothers rebelled and insisted on three strikes or none. Surprisingly enough he did as well on three strikes as he had done on four. He had overcome the need for a subsidy!

Our country today is full of people who want four strikes. The labor lobby in Washington wants four strikes for labor against three for industry. The manufacturers would get four strikes to labor's three if they could. Farmers want four strikes against three for the consumers. Renters want four strikes against three for owners. Manufacturers want four strike tariffs against three strikes for foreign competition. The four-strike complex, however, is becoming an embarrassment to a deficit-bound federal budget. The trouble is that the four strikes have become a vested right. Nobody wants to play the game on even terms.

The tragedy of our revolt against personal responsibility is that we are becoming less and less competent to bear the burden of our freedom. We rely less and less on ourselves as co-workers with God and more and more upon the patronage of an omnipotent state. We are inviting bondage by our revolt against individual responsibility. The time has come for a decisive change of psychological climate if we are to emerge from the morass of the present into a brave new world of freedom and promise. We had better recapture the mood of the rower who knows full well that if the race is to be won, "Every man must pull his own weight and a little bit more."

III

There is, then, a third assumption of democracy, undergirding our freedom "under God." It has to do with the "little bit more" than ourselves that we are expected to pull. It is something of a paradox, I know, to say that "every man must pull his own weight," and then to add the admonition of St. Paul: "Bear ye one another's burdens, and so fulfil the law of Christ." Nevertheless, the paradox is a creative one. To ignore the paradox is to invite the failure of democracy. We are persuaded that every man ought to bear his own burdens, but in our modern industrial society there are many who cannot bear their own burdens. They, the weak, are the responsibility of the strong.

What troubles me is the disposition of so many of those of us who are able to pull our own weight to ignore the needs of those who cannot. We do not want large-scale federal housing, but we propose no other means for housing the "ill housed." We do not want socialized medicine, but we have not strenuously exerted ourselves to find some way to make adequate medical care available to the multitudes who are unable to have it now. There is a parable, a disturbing parable, of our behavior in the story John M. Wilson tells of the glowworms in Waitoma Cave, a great limestone cavern in New Zealand. The cave is inhabited by a galaxy of tiny glowworms that attach themselves to the roof and walls of the cave. The glowworms, larvae of a small fly found only in New Zealand, are not there merely to enchant the tourist. They are busy fishing in the air for insect food. As they fish, their lights shine. The radiance of each little light is in direct proportion to the hunger of the glowworm. The hungrier the glowworm, the brighter is his light. He spins and lets down fine glutinous threads from the roof of the cave. When a gnat or other small insect, attracted by the light, collides with one of these strange fishing lines, it is caught and held. The glowworm reels in the line and consumes the captive. When its hunger is so satisfied, the glowworm puts out his light. The soft lights that give the Glowworm Grotto its unearthly beauty are not produced by contented glowworms. The lights come from glowworms that are hungry and in dead earnest about their fishing.

There is a human analogy in this description of glowworm behavior. With us, as with them, comfort too often brings complacency in its wake. Satisfied and comfortable our lights go out and we ignore the needs of those who still are hungry or hurt or in despair. Intent upon remaining comfortable we resent the struggles of the uncomfortable and accept all too little responsibility for their needs. But the Christian faith rightly insists that society cannot be free unless society becomes a community of the socially concerned. We are "bound in the bundle of life" one with another, or as Walt Whitman said, we are "the clutch'd together." We all need one another and we cannot "live alone and like it." Indeed, we cannot live alone at all because we are bound together, life with life, and fate with fate. Trouble anywhere begets trouble everywhere. Hunger anywhere is a peril everywhere. We are in fact a neighborhood, but we are by no means a community of the concerned. On the contrary, we are a chaos of conflicting interests largely unrelieved by compassion.

"Under God" we are one brotherhood, admonished to "bear ye one another's burdens." We need to understand that it is only "where the spirit of the Lord is," creating socially responsible citizens, that freedom is possible. Only under allegiance to God do we become socially sensitive, responsible citizens; under the sovereignty of the secular we are irresponsible, inviting the regimentation we resent.

Under God we become morally responsible; under the sovereignty of the secular we remain irresponsible. Under God we can pull our own weight, and more; under the sovereignty of the secular we are forever wanting four strikes and something for nothing. As Joshua said to the children of Israel: "Choose you this day whom you will serve."

A BRIDGE TO SPAN THE TIDE

And the king said, "Is the young man Absalom safe?
II SAMUEL 18:29

REVOLT WAS IN THE AIR. ANYBODY COULD FEEL IT, THOUGH IT WAS not easy to find the source of it. David was growing old and it seemed obvious to some of the enlightened members of the younger generation that the nation needed a change. The king still believed in the old-fashioned virtues of the "good old days," and the older he grew, the more cautious he became. Absalom did the best he could to enlighten his aged father, but it seemed to him that David simply had lived too long. It was time for a younger hand to take over the leadership of the nation, Absalom thought, but he was depressed by the realization that old though his father was, he was disgustingly healthy and vigorous.

Absalom covered his trail well and few suspected his intrigues. He knew how to use his attractive personality for all it was worth and his ingratiating ways made him popular everywhere. The fact that he was David's son gave him access to the "right people" and enabled him to sidetrack the suspicion that might have fallen upon him. All in all, Absalom cut no mean figure in his father's kingdom.

When Absalom finally showed his hand, much to his father's amazement, it was almost too late to save the kingdom. David and his servants fled from Jerusalem while his captains rallied the loyal remnants of the army. Perhaps it was overconfidence or an excessive estimate of his military genius that led to Absalom's disaster, but in any event, his armies were defeated and he lost his life.

Then there follows one of the most dramatic incidents in the Old Testament. Joab, the king's captain, sent Ahimaaz, a runner, from the battlefield to the king to inform him that Absalom was dead. David was watching for the messenger, who, when he arrived, was startled by the king's first question: "Is the young man, Absalom, safe?" The question was so eager, so anguished, that Ahimaaz had not the courage to tell the truth. He retreated behind a halfhearted evasion. A second runner, however, broke the old man's heart with the callous and exultant announcement that Absalom was dead. Weeping, David cried out: "O Absalom, my son, my son, would I had died for thee."

I

"Is the young man Absalom safe?" The question should have occurred to David long before it did. Absalom had been playing with fire for years and anybody should have been able to see that he was riding for a fall. Pride, self-will, ruthless ambition, lack of integrity—these were forerunners of disaster and David should have known it. The valiant faith and the striking idealism that had made David great laid no claim upon his son. The stirring traditions of Israel and the spiritual heritage of the nation meant nothing to Absalom; he could sweep away the glory of the past without a qualm.

That always is the danger of youth. Its memory is too short to encompass its heritage. Patrick Henry now is only a name and what George Washington stood for is obscured by the shadows of time. The Pilgrims, whose stuffy Puritan conscience has fallen out of favor, no longer stand as heroes

> Whose stern, impassioned stress
> A thoroughfare for freedom beat
> Across the wilderness!

Traditions, however noble, are to be taken with a grain of salt, and yesterday's ideals and values are greeted with a touch of cynicism.

Anybody who wants to start a new movement starts with youth because youth has so much less to forget than age. Youth has not lived long enough to be really sold on its heritage, so its roots are easily dislodged. What is more, youth is daring, venturing where angels fear to tread; and youth is enthusiastic. Way back in the first century, Josephus, the great Jewish historian, wrote the story of the Maccabean revolt which brought disaster upon the Jewish people. His comment on the dynamic behind the philosophy of revolt sounds like a sentence from the morning paper: "It was chiefly the enthusiasm of youth for this doctrine that was responsible for the nation's ruin."

Perhaps a century hence some student of our times will say what Josephus said, and with good reason. The Black Shirts of Mussolini, who marched on Rome and captured the city with their enthusiasm for Fascism, were young men. The Brown Shirts who swept across Germany like a prairie fire were young men, whose enthusiasm for the Nazi creed brought tragedy to their country and disaster to the world. The Communists who conquered Russia were not old men, tired by the struggle for life where life was difficult; they were young men with the promise of the years ahead of them.

We ought to know what Josephus was talking about, for we are living in a world half destroyed, hungry and wounded by the enthusiasm of youth for false doctrines. What has happened, however, is by no means entirely the fault of youth. The young men who flaunt the communist banners were born into a world in which old faiths were dead and traditional loyalties scorned in the councils of men. They grew to maturity in a world that had lost its soul; among men and women who had forgotten the meaning of life. They took their directions from a generation that was lost, a generation whose faiths had been shattered by war and whose values has been scuttled by defeat, depression and despair. Then, when the tides began to run and new forces, malignant and demonic, swirled around their feet, they were caught. They had no faith, no high purpose, no all-embracing ideals with which to span the tide.

There is no use looking smugly at ourselves now in our triumphant power and saying: "It Can't Happen Here." It can. That is the realistic fact of the matter. It can—unless the roots of youth go deeply into its heritage, unless its ideals are anchored in a steady faith, unless its loyalties can span the tide that threatens. Much depends upon that "unless." It suggests that it need not happen here, and that we should be able to give a new twist to the words of Josephus and leave it for the future historian to say: "It was chiefly the enthusiasm of youth for its heritage that was responsible for the nation's salvation."

It should be clear now, when the tides are running against the things that make life worth living, that we ought to be asking: "Is the young man Absalom safe?"

II

Clearly he is not safe, and neither are we unless his idealism can bridge the tide that is running so savagely against the ancient, well-tried traditions of right and wrong. War, cold war and ideological conflicts breed a mood unfriendly to ideals and leave behind a legacy of moral rot. Truth is no virtue while the nations rage and lies are clothed as virtues if they deceive the enemies we hate. Fraud and violence come into their own to be blessed and crowned. Deception is practiced on a scale undreamed, and purity becomes the virtue of the fool, the crowning stupidity of the "timid soul." A whole generation is taught that the virtues of Christianity are sheer weakness.

When the clock runs wild, in defiance of the stream of time, we simply set it back and then adjust the lever to keep it moving with the sun. But life will not turn back. The cynicism of our moral code in the international struggle for power is like a cancerous growth that pushes its poison into our common life. It is like a clock run wild until no man knows the time of day or night. After World War I we sang a song called "I'm Running Wild," and so we did. As one senator remarked, we seemed to think that "the recording angel had gone on a protracted vacation." He added as an afterthought that we probably had decided there really was no recording angel.

Since the end of World War II, after Nagasaki and Hiroshima, we are wondering if Christianity has any place amidst the ghastly crimes of men. We wonder what we can believe and trust and if the virtues of our better days are sound. But we must know and Absalom must know. When the world is upside down the way it is, a man has to know in his own soul just where he stands and what he believes. A very skillful gymnasium teacher put the matter wisely when he was teaching a class of boys to tumble, turn somersaults in the air and handsprings backward and forward. When one of the boys fell heavily, the teacher shook his head and remarked, "You've got to know where you are when you're upside down." That's what we must know now; where we stand, what we believe, when the world is upside down and the values we have trusted are being swept away by the tide.

You will know where you stand and what ideals you can trust; you will know where you are in this twisted world if you have traveled with Christ and if he has mastered your mind and haunted your heart. In him you will see that back of what is good and noble and honest and true, there is the strength of the imperishable spirit of God. He will show you a cross and you will listen to the mocking laughter of those who thought they had won—had finished him forever. Then he will ask your conscience, "Do you think they really won?"

"Is the young man Absalom safe?" If he has learned from the Master what ideals he can trust, his enthusiasm for his moral heritage may yet be responsible for the nation's salvation and for his own as well. His bridge will span the tide of tumult in our time and bear him to a better tomorrow.

III

The tide is running violently against another aspect of the heritage of youth—against the self-reliance that sent the covered wagons across a continental wilderness and hewed a thoroughfare from the Atlantic to the Pacific. Self-reliant thoughtfulness wrought the intellectual "flowering of New England" and the spiritual genius of Boston and Cambridge and Concord. The self-reliant courage of the pioneers caused the desert to bloom like a rose and alabaster cities to push their spires above the prairies and plains.

Now a new mood is upon us and a new tide is tugging at our feet. We want to be coddled and pampered and carried along, as if the world owed us a living. We can lean on our shovels and loaf on our jobs and collect unearned pay without blinking. The thrift and the industry that drove our fathers toward independence have "gone with the wind" and the tide. We do not even think for ourselves. Television and radio save us that trouble. We want security without struggle, comfort without conquest, ease without effort.

The mood is a dangerous one on which to nourish Absalom. The world owes no man a living unless he has shouldered his own responsibility and done his best to bear the burden of himself. There is a striking sentence in the book of Nehemiah at the end of the triumphant story of the men and women who built the walls around the city of Jerusalem to make the Holy City secure against enemies round about. Nehemiah says proudly, "We built the wall; and all the wall was joined together . . . : for the people had a mind to work." Let no man minimize the significance of that mood. Be men rich or poor, laborers or captains of industry, there is no substitute for "the mind to work" if we would build a nobler future for the generations yet unborn. Langston Hughes, the Negro poet, has it right when he says:

Labor! Out of labor came the villages
And the towns that grew to cities.
Labor! Out of labor came the rowboats
And the sailboats and the steamboats,
Came the wagons and the coaches,
Covered wagons, stage coaches,
Out of labor came the factories,
Came the foundries, came the railroads.

. . . .

Out of labor—white hands and black hands—
Came the dream, the strength, the will,
And the way to build America.[1]

The song is growing older now, but we still feel a thrill when we sing "God Bless America." We forget, however, that the blessing, if it comes, will be an achievement, not a gift. We have the gift— green fields, fertile acres, forests of trees, sun, wind and rain—the rest is up to us. Our fathers put their hands to their plows and spent their lives and strength abuilding. They shouldered responsibility for themselves, and for a little bit more than themselves, or they would not have left us "the land of the free and the home of the brave."

"Is the young man Absalom safe?" Not unless he has learned that in the economy of God every man must pull his own weight and a little bit more. If he knows that and spends his life living out the philosophy of it, it may yet be said of our times that the enthusiasm of youth for this doctrine was responsible for the nation's salvation.

IV

While the tide runs against the great traditions of right and wrong and against our heritage of self-reliance, it is running, too, against the faith of our fathers. That faith meant everything to the little band of Pilgrims who anchored their fortunes to the soil near

[1] *Labor*, by Langston Hughes, Musette Publishers, Inc., N. Y.

Plymouth Rock. They risked their lives to keep it and to bequeath it to their children. They were not fooling when they said they would rather die than do without it, so it is no wonder that their faith plowed itself into the life of New England and the nation.

At the heart of that faith was a confidence in the availability of God anytime, anywhere. Emerson had the faith, and what he wrote breathes the spirit of the God he found in the silence he loved: Thoreau had it, and his *Walden* is alive with the God of the hills and the streams: Bronson Alcott shared it, and his lectures are vivid with the grace of God which he felt wherever two or three were gathered together.

Maybe we are coming to seek God now, I am not sure, but I think there are signs abroad that both youth and its elders are feeling the need for God more keenly than for some time past. War made us see what men can be and do and made us conscious of our spiritual need if we would be the men God meant. Present unrest, anxiety and strain have opened our eyes to the fact we need sources of stability and strength beyond ourselves. Those who dare to think have come to understand that life must take a deeper tone or else go down in the storm.

If Absalom has come to that conclusion, he is on the right track. If he is sending his roots down into God, he will not blow down when the hurricane roars overhead and the tide tears at his feet. If he understands, as Goethe said, that "what your fathers won, you must earn for yourselves," he will dig deeper yet. Then he will stand, knowing within that the great Other walks at his side calling above the storms: "My strength is made perfect in weakness, so just hold on." If Absalom holds fast while the tide swirls about him it may yet be said that his anchorage in the faith of his fathers was responsible for the nation's salvation.

"Is the young man Absalom safe?"

Concerning Ourselves

→»×«←

Men at some time are masters of their fates:
The fault, dear Brutus, is not in our stars,
But in ourselves, that we are underlings.
William Shakespeare, *Julius Caesar*

THREE MEN WITH A CHANCE

☙

And unto one he gave five talents, to another two, and to
another one; to every man according to his several ability.

MATTHEW 25:15

☙

JESUS NEVER TRIED TO EVADE UNPLEASANT FACTS OR DIFFICULT PROB-
lems. He faced them squarely and as a consequence the gospels
contain what scholars are disposed to call "the hard sayings of
Jesus." There are, for example, two sentences in the parable of the
talents that have a disconcerting ring. The first one comes at the
beginning of the story. A man, "traveling into a far country," Jesus
said, "called his servants and delivered unto them his goods." That
seems reasonable enough. Someone had to manage affairs while the
traveler was gone. But then comes the disturbing sentence: "And
unto one he gave five talents, to another two, and to another one;
to every man according to his several ability." A talent represented
approximately one thousand dollars.

At a time when we are talking in terms of social and economic
equality and the Communists are winning the world with their in-
sistence on equality in theory if not in practice, that sentence is upsetting. But Jesus had no illusions and he knew full well that all
men are not created equal. To be sure, in a democracy we are equals
before the law and under God no man is better than any other man,

but we are not equal in talent, capacity or ability. We scarcely could be more unequal.

When we come to the end of the parable, there is another sentence that seems even more distressing. The traveler has come home and the servants are reporting on their stewardship. The servant with five talents had accumulated five more, and the servant with two had doubled his. The man with one talent, however, had buried his talent and now he returned what he had received exactly as his employer had delivered it to him. Jesus denounced the one-talent man; took what he had from him and gave it to the man who had turned his five talents into ten. Then comes the upsetting sentence: "For whosoever hath, to him shall be given, and he shall have more abundance: but whosoever hath not, from him shall be taken away even that he hath."

I

On the face of it, these two sentences seem to contradict the "love one another" spirit of the gospels. They apparently sustain a "dog eat dog" philosophy of rugged individualism wherein the rich get rich and the poor get poorer. But when you get to the heart of the parable there is no such implication in it. Jesus never encouraged anybody to plunder the poor and he never encouraged economic injustice. He simply stated a law of life, and he began with the facts.

The principle is very simple. It is suggested by the title of a radio program wherein people get prizes for answering foolish questions that nobody with good sense would want to ask in the first place. The principle I am talking about is not in the program, but in the title! "Double or Nothing." The title is the final summing up of a law of life and it is the key to the parable and to the two hard sayings of Jesus that are embedded in it.

Jesus began with the assumption that each of us is the care-taker of at least one gift of God. Every man has a minimum of one talent. Some have two talents and some have five, but all of us are equal in one thing—the power to double what we have. When it comes to multiplying our talents, we all have an equal chance. Actually, Jesus might have turned the parable around and put it in reverse so that the one-talent man doubled his talent and the five-talent man buried his. In life it often happens that way. The fact that a man is gifted does not guarantee that he will multiply his capacities. He may very well rest on his laurels.

In life it is a case of "Double or Nothing," use it or lose it. Years ago a reporter interviewed Fritz Kreisler, the great violinist, after he had given a recital in Kansas City. The reporter remarked, "You must be very grateful for talent such as yours." He replied with a twinkle in his eye: "Yes, I am grateful for my talent, but it keeps me pinned down. Having talent is like having a dog, you have to keep exercising him or his muscles turn to fat." So, talent, native ability, is a gift in the beginning, but it has to be multiplied or it gets mildewed. In the end it is "Double or Nothing."

You know from your own experience that your gifts become rusty when you fail to use them. An elderly lady put the matter plainly. She had been ill and had taken up knitting to help pass the time of her convalescence. "I haven't done any knitting for years," she remarked, "and all my fingers feel like thumbs." Obviously you cannot save your talent by conserving it. Sometimes I think students in high school and college work on the assumption that mental powers are conserved by not taxing them overmuch!

Actually the more you tax a talent the more you multiply it. F. Scott Fitzgerald, who began his career of writing with so much promise in the twenties, lost most of his genius because, as he said, "I have been a poor caretaker of my talent." But no man or woman has any business being a poor caretaker of God's gift. It makes no difference whether you are a one-talent man or a five-talent man, the principle holds, "Double or Nothing," and anyone is a fool to make nothing of something.

In the parable of the talents, God gave three men a chance, each "according to his several ability." Two of them doubled what God gave them; the third left his talent unused and got nothing. Three men were exactly equal in the chance God gave them. One man missed his chance.

II

The key to the one man's failure is to be found in a single sentence. Said he, in explaining why he had buried his talent, "I was afraid." That, of course, is a common human failing. Being afraid, we accentuate the negative and minimize the positive in our situation. We count up all our liabilities and forget to add up our assets. Actually almost anybody can give himself a bad case of discouragement and inferiority by focusing attention on his weaknesses. There are so many things I cannot do, that I have to keep my mind on what I can do or I would lose all confidence in myself.

One of your major problems is to accentuate your assets and another is to overcome your liabilities. Take the matter of personal appearance. If you have a homely face you do not need to accentuate your weakness by wearing a hairdo reminiscent of the Gay Nineties and a hat that looks as if it came from the missionary barrel. No, you compensate for your inadequate face by making the best of the rest of you. You can dress with taste and cultivate an inner radiance to the point where your face is by no means a liability.

Maybe you have a one-talent mind, the plodding sort. It takes you two hours to learn what your neighbor with an I.Q. of 140 can learn in half an hour. But certainly you can compensate with tenacity for what you lack in speed. There is more than a little wisdom in the old story of the hare and the tortoise. The tortoise could not run, but at least he could keep on going while the hare was napping. He compensated for the lack of speed with persistence. And, let it be noted, the world is full of men and women with one-talent minds and tenacity who are pushing far ahead of men and women with five-talent minds who are napping.

You never need to be afraid if you will focus on your assets and at the same time work to overcome liabilities. God does not love you any less because you have a second-rate mind. On the contrary, he can use a second-rate mind with first-rate results. Stanley Baldwin, one-time British prime minister, once described how he failed in the entrance examinations for the Fourth Room at Harrow. He was disappointed, but he says, "I got over it in subsequent years when I learned that two of the most distinguished men in public life today had shared my fate." Now, of course, I do not recommend failure in college entrance examinations as a prerequisite to success. What I want to suggest is that despite his intellectual limitations, Stanley Baldwin so thoroughly flogged and pushed his mediocre mind that he was quite able to hold his own and more with men ten times as gifted as he. By relentless discipline, he doubled what he had as a native talent. By way of self-discipline he compensated for his liability and turned it into an asset.

Quite possibly you do not have what it takes to be the star of the play, but you may be invaluable in the supporting parts where God needs you. Where would Abbott be without Costello, and where would Jerry Lewis be without Dean Martin. If you can't be a star, be a foil. A lad at a prep school had the idea when he wrote home to his father: "Dear Dad, I'm having a wonderful time playing football. I'm the second-string half-back on the third team."

You may be only a "second-string half-back on the third team," but you can keep on playing the game, putting your best into it and making the most of the talent you have. The letter you win or the honor of being a star is not half so important as getting the best there is out of you. The sad part of life is that so many people feel they don't amount to much so they go to seed. They are afraid they are inadequate so they never discover how much they can accomplish with what talent they have.

I thought of that the other day when my mind was on a tour for a helpful illustration and I recalled a vaudeville violinist I saw years ago. He was a comedian and he was playing "Turkey in the Straw" with variations. Evidently he had a concealed wire cutter attached to the violin, because as he was playing, the first string snapped. He went on playing on the next string without a stop. Then the second string broke with a pop, and he shifted his attention to the third string. When that string let go, he finished playing on one string and ended with a flourish. The point is that he made music on only one string. And so you can make unsuspected music on one string if you approach that string with confidence, not fear. Believe in your assets, even if you have only one string.

If you are going to make the most of your talents you have to start, of course, with faith in your known assets and without fear of your inadequacies. It is important also to recognize that there are talents and capacities in you that you have not yet discovered. God has given you a multitude of hidden assets. The three men who were given a chance to prove themselves had no idea what would come of their opportunity. Two of them, however, believed in the possibilities, believed they could create something beyond what they had when they started. The third man looked upon his one talent as a dead-end street wherein there was nothing more to be discovered.

No matter who you are, there is more to you than you have yet discovered. A young man expressed the idea the other day when we were talking about Albert Schweitzer, probably the outstanding mutliple-talent man of our day. He is a great musician, theologian, philosopher and surgeon. The young man observed, "I have no doubt there are not a few men and women equipped with native abilities equal to those of Dr. Schweitzer. The trouble is that most of us will not pay the price he paid." Precisely so. There is more ability and talent in you than you have been willing to toil to make available.

It is plain from the parable of the talents that God expects you to discover your hidden assets and make the most of them. Christianity allows no man to rest content with the mediocre when the better and the best are possible.

III

That leads us to the conclusion of the matter, to the fact that talents and powers flower only in response to a motive big enough to lure them to the surface. The parable clearly implies that the two zealous servants were motivated by an overpowering desire to please the man who gave the talents and offered them their chance. Certainly the word of the Master to the zealous servants indicates his delight. Said he, "Well done, thou good and faithful servant: thou hast been faithful over a few things, I will make thee ruler over many things: enter thou into the joy of thy Lord." Notice, if you will, that the profit motive was not a primary concern. The journeying king simply made his three servants trustees over a portion of his wealth. The motive for good stewardship was a will to please the king.

So, in our lives, there is no motive more glorious or more potent than the will to please the King. As our Confession of Faith has it, "The chief end of man is to glorify God." What is more, we glorify Him simply by making the most of ourselves for His sake. We please the Father by our devotion to beauty and truth, goodness and love, by using our minds and our talents in the service of the highest values we know. We honor God as we reach beyond our grasp and aim at heights beyond where we are.

What troubles me about our times is that we seem to fear the heights. After interviewing hundreds of students from the college graduating classes of 1952, Penn Kimball remarked that most of them are looking for comfortable berths with a maximum of security. Said he, "The graduating student appears to be staring straight ahead, rather than upward. He talks about exploring plateaus, not peaks."

But plateaus do not multiply talents, peaks do. It is the heights we see ahead that challenge our powers and stir our talents. Paul never would have been Paul without the peak that lured him from Tarsus to Jerusalem, and from Jerusalem to Athens. He saw in the dim distance "a city not made with hands, eternal in the heavens." It was the summation of all Jesus meant by the "kingdom of God." He took grave risks to scale the peak that reached above the clouds, but how he multiplied his powers as he climbed. To all appearances he was not much of a man, but he used all of him there was, mind and body and spirit. What made Paul the man he was was the motive that lifted him above his fears, and above himself.

It is our self-consciousness that makes us afraid to try our talents. Watch a self-conscious child sitting down at the piano to play for guests. She would give anything to escape, not because she wishes to be contrary, but rather because she is afraid of making a poor impression. Good causes suffer repeatedly because self-conscious people are afraid to risk their talents. They are afraid of failure. Through the years I have listened to a considerable number of seminary students preaching experimental sermons. Most of them are understandably ill at ease; but now and then one of them catches fire. He becomes not a student preacher, self-consciously on trial; but a passionate preacher of great convictions anchored in the Word of God. He becomes the servant of a message and all of the hidden powers of his mind and spirit flower.

Life is like that. It was so with Lincoln. Benjamin Thomas notes wisely that Lincoln's greatness rested not on uncommon abilities, but rather on the moral passion that tied them together. His power rested "on his conviction that nothing less than the universal liberty of mankind was a goal worthy of a great people." He was awkward, ill at ease and unsure of himself until he sensed in a profound way that God was using him to accomplish a great purpose. His powers multiplied in response to a challenge from beyond himself. Why should he be afraid? What happened to him was of little moment beside what happened to God's dream of the "universal liberty of all mankind."

Three men began with a chance. The alternative was plain: "Double or Nothing." You and I stand today where those three men stood, with five, two, or one talent in hand. Now as then the alternative is plain: "Double or Nothing."

DOING WHAT YOU'D
RATHER NOT

I delight to do thy will, O my God: yea, thy law is within
my heart.   PSALM 40:8

THERE ARE TWO PHRASES THAT CHARACTERIZE OUR NORMAL RESPONSE
to outward circumstances or inner imperatives which require
us to do what we would rather not. In all probability we say to ourselves and perhaps to others, "I don't want to," and then we follow
that sentiment with a counterproposition, "I would rather." Those
two phrases summarize our fundamental feeling when we ought to
do what we prefer not to do. Nevertheless, as Immanuel Kant, the
great German philosopher, noted, we are far more likely to be right
when we are doing what we would rather not than when we are
doing what we want to do.

Usually we know what we ought to do in given situations. The
Psalmist put it bluntly when he wrote: "Thy law is within my
heart." That inner law we cannot escape. The problem is to enjoy
fulfilling the demands of the inner law. Portia gave voice to the
problem in *The Merchant of Venice* when she observed: "If to do
were as easy as to know what were good to do, chapels had been
churches and poor men's cottages princes' palaces." John Drinkwater sounded a similar note in his poem-prayer which ends with
the lines:

Knowledge we ask not, knowledge Thou hast lent,
But, Lord, the will, there lies our deepest need,
Give us to build above the deep intent
The deed, the deed.[1]

So, our problem is to do as well as we know even when we would
rather not; it is to unite the will and the inner law and to say: "I delight to do thy will, O my God: yea, thy law is within my heart."

I

When we consider our own experience it is clear that all too
easily "I don't want to" turns into the decision, "I won't," and we
take the road of rebellion against the highest we know. Gertrude
Stein used to say that the "lost generation" of the twenties was a
generation in revolt against moral discipline. Multitudes seemed to
be saying then, as now, "I don't want to be good," having come to
the conclusion that "honesty, industry and integrity don't get you
to the top any more." We sang a song called "I'm Runnin' Wild"
and it expressed our mood. Discipline was a word we did not like
because discipline involved taking ourselves in hand and doing
what we would rather not. Duty was another word that ran counter
to our mood because it involved surrendering our desires on the
altar of our obligations.

Twenty years ago Albert Schweitzer noted that our lack of moral
discipline was undermining the foundations of our civilization and
Arnold Toynbee is saying now that we must choose between discipline and disaster. It is an ominous choice, but the truth is all too
obvious when we consider the events of our time. All too long we
have been saying "I don't want to," "I won't" to the fundamental
integrities upon which our civilization rests. Generation after generation business said "I won't be fair" to the legitimate demands of
labor; and now much too often labor is saying the same thing in

---

[1] "A Prayer" from *Poems 1908–1919*. Copyright, 1919, by John Drinkwater and
used by permission of Samuel French, Ltd.

answer to business. Ever since the end of World War II we have been saying to the world, "We won't stick to our principles if our principles seem to run counter to our interests." We should not be surprised if the world has lost faith in our integrity and now questions our right to moral leadership.

The difficulty is that when we take the road of rebellion against the inner law, we invariably get lost. We find no peace even when we have done what we thought we wanted to do. We blunder into the predicament of a small girl whose mother told her one morning to clear the breakfast table: "I don't want to," came the reply. "Well, then," said the mother, "pick up the papers from the floor." Again the reply: "I don't want to." Her mother, busy, hurrying to go to the grocery, said: "All right, then, do what you want to do." To which the little girl replied in a vexed tone: "I don't want to do what I want to do." So it is that our rebellion against our duties and our moral obligations leads us to uncreative dead ends wherein nothing we want to do gives us any satisfaction.

Unhappily, the world is full of men and women in revolt against the demands of necessity and the inner compulsions of God. There are men and women in revolt against the discipline of monogamy, striking out against what they regard as the tyranny of their self-imposed responsibility for a home and children. The sordid stories of their infidelities fill the newspapers and the pulp magazines. Their infidelity is the symbol of their revolt. There are men and women in revolt against the discipline of honest toil. Without pride in fine workmanship, they cannot obey the summons: "Whatsoever thy hand findeth to do, do it with all thy might." Their shoddy workmanship is the testament of their rebellion.

Nevertheless, "thy law is within my heart," and we cannot escape the gnawing imperatives within that summon us to do the best we know regardless of our wishes. Our restlessness is the price we pay for our rebellion. Our inward conflicts are the evidence of our failure to do as well as we know. The dramatic story of Jonah is a parable of our plight. God summoned Jonah to preach at Nineveh, but Jonah, knowing full well what he ought to do, had no wish to do it. His revolt was complete and final. "I won't," he said to himself as he boarded a ship for Tarshish, as far from Nineveh as he could get. But the story of his three-day journey in the belly of a whale is only a fabulous account of an inner experience, an eloquent way of saying that no man can escape the necessity for doing what he would rather not, if he ought to do it. The whale, you will remember, took Jonah to Nineveh, where he should have gone in the first place.

Most of us are in revolt one way or another most of the time. We hear the voice of God speaking to us through the imperatives of a conscience enlightened by our vision of Jesus Christ, but we say: "I don't want to." "I won't." "I would rather." So we do as we please. Then, not even God can give us peace. Not all the angels and archangels can save us from our inner conflicts and miseries.

II

If we do not take the road of rebellion when we face the imperatives of God implicit in our situation, quite possibly we take the road of resentful acquiescence. We do what we would rather not, but we do it with poor grace. We are somewhat like a boy I watched once as he pushed a lawnmower in the hot sun. Obviously he was doing what he had no wish to do. He acted as if he had a major grudge against the lawnmower. He would push it viciously into the grass, jerk it back and push again. The set of his face and every angry gesture told the world he was cutting the lawn under protest. That evening I saw the boy at a picnic and said in fun: "I am glad the spirit moved you to cut the lawn today." He answered with an engaging grin: "The spirit did not move me. My mother did."

On every street there are men and women who are doing what they would rather not resentfully. They cannot say: "I delight to do thy Will, O my God." On the contrary, like the Psalmist in his weariness they complain, "How long, O Lord, how long?" They do what they must simply because they must. There are, for example, young people who want to be free to marry and build homes of their own, but they are burdened with responsibility for parents or brothers or sisters. They do what they know they must, but they do it resentfully. They fret and complain and bore others with their complaints. There are men who are pulling heavy loads, trying to support their families on inadequate incomes, bitterly resenting their difficulties and leaving trails of fretting and complaint wherever they go. Their feeling is by no means difficult to understand, but it leaves them without a chance for creative, vital living.

The truth is that no man escapes situations in which he is compelled to go on and on doing what he would rather not, bearing burdens he would rather drop. What happens to him under the stress of necessity, however, depends upon himself. Consider the experience of Handel, writing *The Messiah* under circumstances he would rather not face. Says his biographer: "His health and his fortunes had reached the lowest ebb. His right side had become paralyzed, and his money was all gone. His creditors seized him and threatened him with imprisonment. For a brief time he was tempted to give up the fight—but then he rebounded again to compose the greatest of his inspirations, the epic Messiah." So, whether the "Hallelujah Chorus" was going to be written depended altogether upon what Handel did with himself in a hopeless situation. Let it be noted that the "Hallelujah Chorus" never could have come from a resentful, bitter mind. It came from a mind that could say: "I delight to do thy will, O my God."

Once, long ago, the people of Israel had come to the end of their rope. They were exiles in a strange land, compelled day by day to do what they would rather not. They were slaves of a conquering people. The prophet Ezekiel was among them. All around him he saw people who were resentful, angry, bitter. Who could blame them? There was no hope. They must go on and on dreaming of

42976

Zion, yet doing what they had no wish to do; wishing for their Holy City, but with no hope of ever going there. They lost faith and hope and their morale was at the bottom. But in the midst of those resentful exiles came a new and decisive factor. Ezekiel put the truth simply and gloriously. Said he: "The spirit entered into me and set me on my feet." So, into the resentment and bitterness of Israel there came a new spirit that transformed drudgery into sublime duty, frustration into fortitude, and gave birth to Israel's insight and spiritual power.

Resentment is a dead-end street that leads nowhere, but there is a spirit that transforms resentment into veritable rejoicing. Bitterness is a blind alley, but by the grace of God we can change blind alleys into highways of hope.

III

That leads us to the third possibility when we confront the necessity of doing what we would rather not. The third road is the road of resignation. It is a road that is littered with self-pity and unutterable sadness. Shakespeare has a word picture of a small boy traveling the road of resignation in his description of the

> . . . whining school-boy with his satchel
> And shining morning face, creeping like a snail
> Unwillingly to school.

There are a hundred things the boy would rather do, but he submits to the inevitable with sad resignation.

Turn anywhere you please and you will see people who have taken the road of resignation. The fight has gone out of them. Day by day they plod without hope. Their dreams have faded into disappointment. They are not happy. Indeed, they have given up expecting to be happy. They do their work reasonably well, but they are like machines, without any heart. They take their disappointments, their sorrows, their hurts with resigned self-pity, as if they were bowing to the will of God. They go along in their accustomed ruts in obedience to fate. But they never get within a country mile of the abundant life Jesus came to bring. They know "thy law is within my heart," but they cannot say: "I delight to do thy will, O my God."

The trouble with the road of resignation is that there is no lift to it. It brings us to the inevitable question: "What's the use?" Why go on doing what we would rather not, plodding without hope? Huckleberry Finn felt the truth in Mark Twain's famous story. Huck was left to shift for himself by a worthless father who slept with the boys in the tanyard and made a living stealing. On one of the numberless occasions when Huck was in trouble, he made this confession: "I see it wan't no use for me to try to learn to do right. . . . What's the use learning to do right when it's troublesome and it ain't no trouble to do wrong?" So, he reckoned he would do "whichever came handiest."

When we have lost our fight on the road of resignation there is not much point in doing what we would rather not. We may as well simply do "whichever comes handiest." The German people took the road of resignation under Hitler and the Italian people took the road of resignation under Mussolini. Today, all over the world in countries behind the Iron Curtain, people are taking the same road, doing whatever "comes handiest," not because they believe what comes handiest is what they ought to do, but because they have lost their fight. They are resigned. Sometimes I have the feeling that we are on the road of resignation, too, wondering what is the use of trying to be Christian, trying to do right, trying to find a way through the world conflicts of today. It is so much easier to do "whichever comes handiest."

IV

There is a fourth road, however, that holds promise. It is the road of rejoicing that transforms what we ought to do into what we want to do. Listen to the Psalmist: "I delight to do thy will, O my

God: yea, thy law is within my heart." "I had rather be a door-keeper in the house of the Lord than to dwell in the tents of wicked-ness." You get the same note in Jesus: "My meat, [my satisfaction, my joy] is to do the will of him that sent me." Immanuel Kant summed up the idea when he wrote that the ultimate task of life is so to identify yourself with your duty that it becomes your in-clination.

Christianity is by no means a matter of trying to be good. It is, as Harry Emerson Fosdick observed, "being good without trying." It is wanting to do what we ought to do because we "love Him who first loved us." It is rejoicing in the chance to do as we ought for Christ's sake. Why should the early Christians endure persecution and agony rejoicing? They wanted to endure hardship as good soldiers of Jesus Christ. How could Clement of Alexandria write in the midst of persecution and tragedy: "Nevertheless, singing we sail: praising we plow." Those early Christians had taken the road of rejoicing, doing what they ought to do for the sheer joy of doing it.

When we are just trying to be good, struggling to make our-selves do what we would rather not, we blunder onto the roads of rebellion, resentment and resignation. But when we catch some trailing of the garment of Christ and sense the wonder of his cross, we can turn off onto the road of rejoicing, to do as we ought be-cause our joy is to do the will of Him that sent us. "I delight to do thy will, O my God" is the endless refrain of the Christian.

Some day we may understand that it is love that transforms duty into desire. It is devotion that turns an obligation into an oblation. George Matheson had it right when he wrote:

> O Love, that wilt not let me go,
> I rest my weary soul in Thee;
> I give Thee back the life I owe,
> That in Thine ocean depths its flow
> May richer, fuller be.

"The life I owe" to Him who loves with an everlasting love is too small a gift to give at best, but it is all I have to give. It is all you have to give, but on the altar of love you and I can give what we have to give and give it rejoicing. We can do the will of God for the sheer joy of doing it. We can say: "I delight to do thy will, O my God: yea, thy law is within my heart."

IT FALLS TO A FEW

And the remnant . . . shall take root downward, and bear fruit upward.　　　　ISAIAH 37:31–35

ISAIAH WAS BRUTALLY HONEST WITH HIS PEOPLE. HE SAW THEM AS they were and he denounced them roundly. "Ah, sinful nation," he shouted, "a people laden with iniquity, a seed of evildoers, children that are corrupters." Then, as if he understood that his people were simply drifting with the tide, and blundering without thinking, he noted sadly, "My people doth not consider." He felt helpless and baffled until he remembered a handful of men and women he called "the remnant." They stood for something, and they would not drift. They still cherished the faith of Abraham and Isaac and Jacob, and they refused to conform to the movement of secular drift. In them Isaiah saw the promise of the future, and with confidence he wrote: "The remnant . . . shall take root downward, and bear fruit upward."

I

Notice the words "shall take root downward." They are decisively important for our time. Certainly, if any one word can describe our era it is the word "uprooted." We have been uprooted geographically. The "displaced persons" of the Old World, men and women without homes or countries, are a symbol of our uprooted age. The home trailer, hitched to an automobile, is another symbol of our rootless, migrant ways. Every year millions move from place to place, from city to city, from apartment to apartment. Nothing is permanent; everything is temporary. The old-fashioned home enduring from generation to generation as a haven of permanent memory has surrendered to the kitchenette with roll-away beds.

Our geographical uprootedness would be no insuperable problem if we had something permanent to tie to, but at the precise time in history when we put ourselves on wheels and wings we also cut our dollars loose from their roots in gold and our morals loose from their roots in God. We set out on a jamboree of economic and moral freewheeling. Nothing much has stayed put and both our dollars and our moral standards have lost their authority. As Gabriel commented in *Green Pastures,* "Everything nailed down is comin' loose." Our fixed points have drifted free from their moorings and left us spinning.

Even our language has been uprooted and common words whose meaning was clear have wandered off the semantic map and lost their grip on the old realities. Take the word "freedom." We know what we mean by it, but Russia uses the same word and it means something else. Or there is the word "democracy." We thought we knew its meaning. Now we are not sure because so many people use the word to describe something we do not mean at all. Almost any word you can mention that bears on ethical or political questions has been uprooted. Truth or justice or right mean different things to different people in our world of conflicting ideologies.

You and I can manage considerable uprootedness if we can hang onto something that has a substantial ring. The behavior of a child when the family is transplanted, moved from one town to another, is revealing. Inevitably he develops a strange attachment. He clings to a particular pillow, a doll, or a dog-eared Teddy bear. The child's attachment may involve almost anything, but it is some-

thing to which he clings in the midst of his uprooting. The battered
Teddy bear is a precious symbol of the familiar. At night, in
strange surroundings he will not go to sleep without it because it
represents a security and continuity with his past.

Our grown-up children who go to college reveal the same phe-
nomenon. They go away from home with a jaunty sense of freedom.
They think it is wonderful to escape their parental apronstrings. No
more do's and don'ts. No more "on the carpet" lectures. But time
changes the perspective. Letters from home seem frightfully important to them. The home they wanted to get away from in
September is the one place they wish to return to in December.
Curiously enough, the relish of going away depends upon the
knowledge that there is a place to which they may return. The
adventure into the new is a joyous experience because there is a
happy avenue of return to the familiar.

One of the loneliest lads I know is in the army now. He is an
orphan and he feels rootless and lost. He will be discharged from
the service some day, but it does not matter too much. He says he
does not care much where he is because he has no place to which he
can return. That, I think, is the essence of being lost: not caring
where you are because there is no secure base that beckons to you to
return. Rootless, you are like a tumbleweed, rolling at random in
response to the winds that blow.

Isaiah saw the "remnant" of his people preserving a place of
moral and spiritual return for a generation adrift. He saw them
rooted downward in the faith of Abraham and Isaac and Jacob,
and "holding fast" to the good in an evil and perverse time. Maybe
the people as a whole were behaving as if the recording angel had
gone on a protracted vacation, but there was hope if a few gallant
souls would hold fast to the decencies the many had forsaken. A
young man summarized the idea when he said: "Some years ago I
left my home on the farm to make my fortune and try my wings.
Fortune eluded me and my wings have been singed like the prodi-

gal son's. Then one Sunday I dropped into your church and there I was reminded of the things I had forgotten. I think I am back on the beam now."

The world is full of uprooted men and women, blowing hither and yon with the wind, following the crowd, blundering into evil, losing their sense of life's meaning. But in the midst of them is the remnant, the creative minority we call the church, holding fast to the things that are good, preserving the ideals and aspirations to which one day they must return. In our uprooted era, men wander far afield, forgetting the best in their heritage, wasting their substance in folly, but so long as the church remains, "holding fast to that which is good," there is hope. So long as there are men and women who sing,

> In the cross of Christ I glory
> Towering o'er the wrecks of time,

and "take root downward" in the cross, there is a chance for a better day.

I am not being sentimental when I say that the significance of the church, preserving a place of spiritual and moral return, cannot be overestimated. It ought to be worth something to you. It ought to be worth your support in terms of generous sacrifice.

II

"And the remnant shall take root downward." It was sheer necessity in Isaiah's day for in the day of adversity, uprooted men are enfeebled by their fears. And it is so in our time. Without roots in the Eternal men and women are beset by fears when they confront a changing, uprooted civilization. Certainly if the first symbol of our generation is the word "uprooted" the second symbol is the frightened rabbit. Herbert Hoover, considering the tragic events of our time, notes rather sadly that we have not behaved rationally since the Great Fear fell upon us with the coming of World War I in 1914.

At Thanksgiving time we sing a great hymn, "Come ye thankful people come," but in our day there is a new note and the church is saying: "Come ye fearful people come," be not afraid. It is a daring word and a needed word. People everywhere are afraid with a nameless fear that eats at their vitals. As a baffled character in a modern novel put it: "There ain't nothin' a body can trust no more." I felt the truth some years ago when a young air force veteran blundered into my office. He had a good job, with nine or ten thousand dollars a year. But, he said, "I can't get over my fears." "What are you afraid of?" I asked him. "My job frightens me. I feel insecure in it, and for no good reason," he answered. "I'm afraid of marriage. I'm just plain afraid." Most of us are afraid too, because we feel insecure. We are uneasy, anxious, troubled.

Our anxiety is not altogether the consequence of circumstances. To be sure, we are worried by the state of the world. Our uprooted, chaotic world makes us anxious. We cannot seem to find a solid footing in the shifting panorama of our upset era. But there is a deeper source of our fears, and it is in ourselves. If we feel inadequate to deal with our circumstances it is because we have no roots to nourish us with resources from beyond ourselves. We are like cut flowers, withering without renewal. We wonder if we can keep up the pace that kills, and stand the strains and tensions we must meet. We wonder if we can endure the uncertainties of the future and come through without coming apart at the seams.

We know full well that we cannot change the circumstances that bear upon us. We cannot "take this sorry scheme of things entire," smash it and rebuild it overnight to our taste. Our problem is to live with the things we cannot change, to find security in the midst of insecurity, and confidence in the heart of confusion. Such was the need of Ezekiel, exiled in Babylon, shaken by the disastrous turn of events that crushed Israel and Judah. But he took root downward, and then remarked: "The spirit entered into me, . . . and set me upon my feet." And Isaiah, confronting national disaster, found security in the midst of it. Said he: "They that wait upon the Lord shall renew their strength." Then, too, there was Paul, meeting situations that would have defeated most of us, but as he said, he was "strengthened with might through His spirit in the inner man."

Our lives need to be fortified and renewed inwardly. We all know that. You know it, and I suspect it is one fundamental reason why you go to church, or feel you ought to go. Your confidence wants renewing. You want to be assured that if hard blows come you can take them and keep on going. You want to know, to be reminded, that the love of God is more than pious sentiment. You want faith big enough and strong enough to deal with your fears. You do not find what you need in your club or your business conventions. No, you know instinctively that in the church you will be "strengthened with might through His Spirit in the inner man." Here you find security in the midst of insecurity, and stability for an unstable time.

So men have discovered in every era. During the days of the Nazi occupation of Norway, when fear swept like a tide over the people, there were multitudes who ran for cover and came to terms with their conquerors. But, in the face of the worst, there were those who were not afraid. They would not compromise and they could not be crushed. Who were they? They were a remnant, a creative minority within the church of Jesus Christ. The Quisling press paid reluctant tribute to them by saying publicly: "The Christian front is the most difficult to conquer." Of course it is the most difficult front to conquer. It cannot be frightened. It has deep roots in the Everlasting.

To be sure, we do not relish grim days even though we have strong roots in God. We do not like the insecurity of a world in unstable equilibrium. We do not relish the need to be hurt or defeated on the altar of our convictions. We regret circumstances that are prophetic of disaster. Jesus did not relish the cross or the need to meet it. "If it be possible," he prayed, "let this cup pass from me." So we pray in our time. "If it be possible" may we be spared the disaster of atomic war, the agony of economic ruin, the tragedy of Communist triumph. "If it be possible, let this cup pass from us."

But there is a sequel to that anguished prayer, and the sequel is the testament of any man's security. After the prayer, "If it be possible, let this cup pass from me," there come the deeper words: "Nevertheless, not my will but Thine be done." Security, salvation from fear, is not in the petition "let this cup pass." No, our salvation is in the "nevertheless," in the knowledge that by God's grace we can take our crosses and transform them into crowns of courage and redeeming loyalty. Our security is in the shining faith that in the hours when worse comes to worst, we are "strengthened with might through His Spirit in the inward man."

In our fearful generation, can you measure the worth of such a faith flowing into the stream of our common life from the creative remnant in the church of Jesus Christ? Can you put a petty price on a faith able to say "Nevertheless" in the face of the worst; a faith nourished and inspired by men and women who "take root downward" and "bear fruit upward" in the life of our time?

III

Clearly the remnant, the creative minority within the church of Jesus Christ, is a bulwark for our times, holding fast to that which is good in our uprooted society and offering a faith big enough to deal with any fear. But taking root downward, that creative minority bears fruit upward by revealing the life of God in the life of their times. There was a time when theologians were accustomed to think of the church as the beloved community of the saved; but now theologians see the church as a saving leaven for society. It is a creative fellowship of men and women pushing out into every facet of society to make it different, to change its spirit with the life of God.

Martin Luther quite literally shook the world when he began to preach "the priesthood of all believers" to a world under the sway of authority. What it did was to fix spiritual responsibility in individuals. When you personalize the doctrine it places moral and spiritual responsibility in your lap. The priest, as Luther saw him, was a servant, a servant of the will of God in society. The priest was a man bearing the life of God into the life of his community. So, if you are part of the creative minority of the church of Jesus Christ you are a man or a woman bearing the life of God into the life of your community, your business, your home or your club. Jesus pointed up the truth when he said: "The kingdom of heaven is like unto leaven, which a woman took, and hid in three measures of meal, till the whole was leavened."

Well, thank God there are men and women who bear the life of God into the life of their times. They are not pious sentimentalists, they are realists whose lives "take root downward and bear fruit upward."

As one man said to me concerning another man: "He is completely incapable of a dishonorable action." That man was bearing the life of God into the life of his times. Or there is a woman I know, bearing the shock of sorrow with dignity and without self-pity. One of her friends said of her: "She is an inspiration." She is bearing the life of God into the life of her day. Or there is a young man, a member of a college fraternity, just standing for something essentially decent, being altogether a man without condescension or pride, and holding weaker men steady just being what he is. That is living the life of God in the life of a college campus.

God will not make the world over without his priests, without men and women "bearing fruit upward" because their roots go downward. I think Robert Nathan caught the truth in his little fantasy, *Mr. Whittle and the Morning Star*. Mr. Whittle, impatient with the world, disgusted by the foibles of his fellows, expects the world soon will be coming to an end. He has a conversation with the Almighty, and he says with impatience: "If it has to be it has to be. It's the waiting around I don't like. Why don't you get it over with?" And God replies, "Don't rush me. I'm trying to think of a way out."

That is not blasphemy. It is an echo from the New Testament, with God using us to find a way out. It is an echo from St. Paul, noting soberly, "We are workers together with God." It is a parable of Luther's conviction that the way out will be clear when we of the creative minority called the church bear the life of God into the life of our times.

When you travel down through the centuries it is plain that those who have "borne fruit upward," revealing the life of God in the life of their day, have been those who "took root downward" by sharing the worship and the fellowship of the Christian community. They found their inspiration there and they were as leaven in three measures of meal. I would hate to live in a world without the remnant in it. I would not wish to live in a community without the leaven flowing into it from the church of Jesus Christ and neither would you.

WHAT MEN NEED MOST

❧

The lord is my shepherd; I shall not want.   PSALM 23:1

❧

BILL MAULDIN, WHOSE CARTOONS MIRRORED THE MIND OF G. I.'S IN action, has gone on interpreting our times in word and picture. He notes with a bit of sadness that we are "the scared-rabbit generation." The description is ominously and disturbingly accurate, as our frantic and unrelenting quest for security suggests all too plainly. We have been uncomfortably off balance since the depression of the thirties upset our neat, serene system and "the good old days" became a nostalgic memory. On the heels of depression came World War II and we worried through that. Then, toward the war's end, we began to be fearful of unemployment and the problems of postwar adjustment. Now we have the cold war and the promise of insecurity for a long time to come. So, we have been and still are living under the tension of our fears and we are indeed "the scared-rabbit generation."

I

Basically we are suffering from want of confidence in anything. I recall years ago visiting the fun house of an amusement park. Things were not what they were alleged to be. Doorknobs responded to my touch with an electric shock. Stairsteps perversely slid out from under me. Streams of compressed air from nowhere blew my hat from my head. An innocent bit of floor suddenly started spinning. By the time I got through the fun house, I was conditioned to mistrust everything. Everything had played me false and left me reeling. We are in somewhat the same predicament now. Things we trusted have played us false. There was a time when we trusted the dollar. A dollar was a dollar any time, anywhere. Now a dollar is not a dollar. We have lost confidence in our political leaders who seem to have lost their way. We have lost confidence in the United Nations and in the possibility of enduring peace. What is worse, we have lost confidence in ourselves and in our significance as makers of history. We have come to the end of our secular tether and at the moment, at least, we are scared rabbits.

Quite possibly the Psalmist had some advantage over us. He lived in a world that moved more slowly than ours. His civilization was not nearly so complex or involved. To be sure, his world was shaken by the clash of empires, Egypt, Babylonia and Assyria were forever on the march, and his little nation was caught in the middle. His land had been ravaged and his cities destroyed again and again. But in the midst of clashing armies and under the threat of disaster, he was steadied by a sure faith that "the Lord is my shepherd; I shall not want. He leadeth me beside still waters; he restoreth my soul." When crises came, he was not a scared rabbit. He was by no means just whistling in the dark to keep up his courage. He had a firm grip on something he could trust. He might be swept into the caldron of war, carried away captive, or crushed beneath the chariots of his conquerors. Nevertheless, he would "fear no evil; for thou art with me." Whatever happened, he could manage for "thy rod and thy staff, they comfort me."

The Psalmist was trying to say that when confidence in everything else is gone, a man can be sure of God. When the secular props for security have been broken, a man can find inner security in God. I think that truth came to the pilot of an American airlines

DC-6 recently when his ship threw a propeller which crashed through the fuselage and ripped the engine from the wing. Flying at twenty-one thousand feet over the Colorado Rockies, the pilot found himself with half the controls gone, but he brought the ship into Denver for an emergency landing. "What do you do when a propeller flies off the airliner you are piloting and rips off half the fuselage?" a newspaper reporter asked. "In a situation like that," the pilot responded, "you just move over a little bit and let God take over."

We have come, in this battered, frightened world of ours, to precisely that point. It is long past time for us to "move over a little bit and let God take over." Perhaps, like Thomas Carlyle, we anchored our lives to a slumbering secular whale that "ducked under and left us spinning in the eddies." At the moment there is not much left to sustain us and see us through. It does not matter, however, if we move over a little to say humbly, "The Lord is my shepherd; I shall not want."

II

Being steadied when we are scared rabbits; finding our way with wisdom when we are under tension requires something more than sleeping pills. The Psalmist has a phrase to describe our deepest need: "He leadeth me beside the still waters." Arnold Toynbee expressed the same idea when he affirmed our abiding need for "withdrawal and return." He notes that the human spirit fails without repeated withdrawal to "the secret place of the most high." His reading of history suggests that we cannot manage the bustle and hurry of Main Street wisely without periodic withdrawal to quietness in order to "see life steadily and see it whole." The

> . . . crowded ways of life
> Where sound the cries of race and clan

are too much for our sanity without renewal "beside still waters."

Jesus withdrew to the wilderness before he "returned unto Galilee in the power of the spirit." So we need to withdraw to the quietness of "still waters" to find our way.

Richard Trench put the truth in lines of power when he wrote:

> Lord, what a change within us one short hour
> Spent in Thy presence will avail to make!
>
> . . . .
>
> We kneel, and all around us seems to lower;
> We rise, and all, the distant and the near,
> Stands forth in sunny outline brave and clear;
> We kneel, how weak! we rise, how full of power!

It is altogether true, and yet we rob ourselves of the insight and the power of withdrawal because we do not often pause to let God lead us "beside the still waters."

At the end of my vacation one summer I spent an hour with the Sunday newspaper. There were news reports of fighting in Korea, a railroad strike unsettled, discord in the United Nations, a murder on Main Street and assorted crimes far and near. Even in the comic section things were wrong. Vitamin Flintheart was in trouble, Red Ryder captured by rustlers and Hopalong Cassidy lost in a sandstorm. What a world! Later that same night I watched a full moon come up over the eastern horizon, peering first through the pine trees and then rising in glory to light the darkened world. Split Rock stood like an enduring sentinel across the valley. Mt. Logan towered majestically above its lesser fellows and the Montezumas in the distance glistened with fresh snow. There was nothing wrong in the nature of things. Things were sublimely right. The moon and the stars moved in obedience to a will more cogent than their own. There was neither confusion nor lostness in the heavens. On the contrary, there was the serenity of perfect order as "the morning stars sang together."

Under the spell of God's beauty there was nothing to fear. The petty anxieties of the day seemed futile within the framework of the night sky. Issues stood out "in sunny outline, brave and clear." There in the quietness I knew the way—the way of obedience to the will of God. If I would let Him guide me, God would order my life as He orders the stars. He would take away my inner dividedness and let my life push on "like a strong, steady wind that blows one way." God would bring peace to the world if men would listen to the voice of His Only Begotten Son. He would bring the "brave new world" of our dreams if we would pause long enough "beside the still waters" to find the way before pressing on.

We blunder into conflict and fear, and things go wrong because we do not seek God's way. The other day a friend of mine remarked that if two people are confronted with exactly the same set of facts they will arrive in due time at the same conclusion. That ought to be true and it would be true if the two people would withdraw into the presence of God to consider the facts. Unfortunately, fears and prejudices and self-interests overwhelm our reason. We think with our emotions instead of our minds. Our unrecognized prejudices undercut our good sense, and we are like the British diplomat, fearful of the power of Napoleon. Said he, quite oblivious to the absurdity of his words: "Thank God I have no prejudices; but God knows I hate a Frenchman." As a nation we are not thinking clearly now. Our fears have warped our intelligence and there is very little evidence anywhere of withdrawal to seek the resources of "still waters" where God's way stands out "in sunny outline, brave and clear." Quite literally we are saying: "Thank God I have no prejudices; but God knows I hate a Communist." Unfortunately, our fear of Communists is making us into dupes. In quest of security we are spending ourselves into insecurity and bankruptcy. In grim pursuit of security we are surrendering our freedom. In terrible search of safety we are yielding to the illusory conviction that military power alone can save us. We forget the warning of Arnold Toynbee that in the light of history, militarism is the last refuge of a morally bankrupt civilization on the road to ruin.

I am not a pacifist, although I have experienced moments of trial
when I have wondered if I ought to be. Nevertheless, I am desperately weary of trying to cure diplomatic dyspepsia with military
medicine. I am weary of trying to undo the moral folly of power
politics with the blood and the broken dreams of young men. I am
sick of listening to nonmoral explanations of China, Korea and
Germany made palatable with a sugar coating of idealism. God give
us men who will withdraw to the "still waters" to find the way
before it is too late.

III

Following the silence of the "still waters" are two sentences in
the 23rd Psalm that are intimately interlinked. Notice the sequence,
for they suggest the same road ahead. Beside the still waters "he
restoreth my soul." Then, with sure confidence the Psalmist goes
on: "He leadeth me in the paths of righteousness, for his name's
sake." It is suggestive that the Hebrew word for "soul" is exactly
the same as the Hebrew word for "breath." Literally, the Psalmist
says: "He restoreth my breath." We might say that He gives us a
second wind to keep us going. It is indeed so. But it is important to
observe that the renewing of our souls, the finding of our second
wind, involves a new-found trust in "the paths of righteousness."

All too frequently we abandon our faith in righteousness beside
the altars of what we call realism. We sell our "moral capital" short
and thereby surrender our souls and our second wind. We put politics before principle and thereby play into the hands of our enemies.
Why do you suppose Russia returned to the Security Council of the
United Nations after a boycott of several months? It is no mystery.
She came back to repair her moral fences in the eyes of the world.
However perverted, twisted and false, her appeal has been to the
right and the just. She has sought by every possible means to prove
the South Koreans the aggressors and to lay the charge of imperial-

ism at the door of the United States. She has demonstrated clearly that no nation dares to be caught wandering off "the paths of righteousness."

Is there any more coercive evidence in the world today that moral power is decisive? Even the immoral pay grudging respect to the moral. Even the vile respect virtue. If they can make the worse appear the better part, that is to the good as they see it, but they cannot escape the moral law of God, "the same yesterday, today and forever." The tragedy is that in our fearfulness we have underestimated the coercive power of righteousness. We have trimmed our sails and hauled in our flags and forgotten our principles. In the years since the war we have followed no less than six different and mutually contradictory foreign policies. Greece and Turkey, Israel and Spain, China and Korea all give evidence of confused thinking. Our fears have robbed us of our principles and left us pawns of power politics until we have lost confidence in everything.

The genius of Abraham Lincoln during the tragic years before and during the Civil War lay in the fact that from beginning to end he was guided by honest principle. His thinking had moral roots. Through defeat and travail he never once lost confidence in the endless power of righteousness and truth. Again and again in crises he moved over a little bit and "let God take over." In the face of every pressure, every criticism, every bitter denunciation he clung to his basic principle—the preservation of the Union. He refused to be lured by side issues or pressed into doctrines of expediency. He would stand or fall beside his basic principle.

What bothers me now is that the only principle that guides us is a negative one—Stop Communism. It is a principle without principle! It has no power to win friends and influence people. Where is the great voice summoning the world to believe in the sacredness of human personality under God? Where are men speaking the truth, the whole truth and nothing but the truth? Where are voices pleading for true freedom under God? Do we now know that in the economy of God

The stars in their courses are one with the forces
That fight for the freedom of men?

In this hour of human destiny we need confidence in the power of righteousness to rule; confidence that under God truth is mightier than the sword. We will not know until we pause beside the still waters to learn that "the Lord is my shepherd; I shall not want."

IV

There is, then, a final word that is important, a promise that in our withdrawal to quietness "beside the still waters" we shall find a new confidence in ourselves as makers of history. We are not ciphers; we are makers of history. The other day I went into a store in the mountains. On the door was a "For Sale" sign. I wandered about, looking on the dusty shelves. Finally the storekeeper remarked: "The trouble is that I have everything that nobody wants." So, the wants of people are the arbiters of a storekeeper's destiny. Likewise, the purposes of men and the actions of men are the arbiters of history. Either we yield to the will of God as revealed in Jesus Christ or our civilization will go out of business.

We have been selling ourselves short, assuming we could not influence the course of events. The Communists are troubled by no such phobias. The young people who gather periodically in Red Square shout in rhythmic chant: "We are changing the world"— and they are. The Christians of the first three centuries never were inhibited by the feeling of futility. They were only a handful, but their persecutors complained that they "upset the world." Like the Communists of today, they believed profoundly in their capacity to determine "the shape of things to come."

It is a thrilling experience to watch boys discovering their powers, little by little disclosing their latent capacities. Day by day they become less dependent and more independent. Today they can do what yesterday they only dreamed of doing; today they are able to climb higher, think straighter, run faster and work more effectively than yesterday. They exert a new influence in the family; become more significant in the social group; touch the life of the community more decisively. They know, in their growing days, that they are by no means nobodies.

Maybe it is the wear and tear of life that reduces us to futility, or possibly we just lose confidence in our capacity to exert influence because we lose confidence in God. Certain it is that the Psalmist and his fellows, nobodies as the Babylonians, Egyptians and Assyrians saw it, were makers of history. Their faith is the warp and woof of our own; their ethic underlay the insights and teachings of Jesus, our Lord. But underneath their confidence in their capacity to make history was their abiding faith: "The Lord is my shepherd; I shall not want." More than all else men need confidence—confidence in God, in righteousness and in themselves as makers of history. It is a confidence born "beside the still waters" with God.

Getting Along at Home

∗≫≪∗

Then homeward all take off their sev'ral way;
The youngling cottagers retire to rest:
The parent pair their secret homage pay,
And proffer up to Heaven the warm request,
That He who stills the raven's clam'rous nest,
And decks the lily fair in flow'ry pride,
Would, in the way His wisdom sees the best,
For them and for their little ones provide;
But chiefly, in their hearts with grace divine preside.

Robert Burns, *The Cotter's Saturday Night*

WHAT RIGHT TO RESPECT?

Honor thy father and thy mother: that thy days may be long upon the land which the Lord thy God giveth thee.

EXODUS 20:12

THE TEN COMMANDMENTS SUGGEST THE CHARACTERISTIC MOVEMENT of Israel's thought from God to man and from eternity to time. The first four commandments have their focus in God as the center of all life and thought. The fifth commandment and those that follow it suggest what the priority of God means in terms of human relationships. In the thinking of Israel God is no absentee landlord hiding in solitary splendor behind a canopy of stars. On the contrary, God is in the very midst of things, involved in our human relations, concerned in our conduct, and interlinked into all of our affairs. The fifth commandment begins where the invasion of God into human life always begins—in our homes.

It was clear to Moses as he sat hammering words upon the tablets of stone that the faith of Israel was transmitted from generation to generation in the tents he could see below him at the foot of Mt. Sinai. There, where parents and children shared life and love, faith was nourished and the heritage of Israel preserved. Whether Israel would be faithful or faithless would be settled there. Quite possibly he felt the tides of revolt in the rising generation. Youth's memory was short, too short to remember what God had done for his people.

So, lest youth forget what age and experience had learned of God, Moses wrote: "Honor thy father and thy mother."

I

In our modern world that is not exactly the custom. There is a suspicion on the part of youth that parents are passé. Young people do not seem much interested in what we did yesterday or why. One evening at our house we were talking about behavior, courtesy and thoughtfulness, and one of the boys asked pointedly: "Say, Mom, did you have any fun back in the Gay Nineties?" I wondered if we seemed that old! It occurred to me then that quite possibly even the Gay Nineties had something to say to our times. Maybe long skirts, tight-fitting trousers, high collars and chaperones have gone out of date, but there remain ideals and values, truths and faiths that are as valid today as they were a thousand years ago. There are some things that remain the same, "yesterday, today and forever." There is chivalry, for example. Chivalry is timeless. The reverence for womanhood that marked the feudal age is forever good; as good now as it ever was. There is integrity, a quality of inner honesty and forthrightness that makes a man thoroughly dependable. When a man has it, his word is as good as his bond. Integrity is as vital now as it was in the Gay Nineties, or in the first century, for that matter.

Sometimes our children have a habit of lumping all of the past—its values and ideals along with high-button shoes—and marking it down as out of date. The time may be coming—I'm not sure—when our children will discover that moral antiques have quality, and what is more, that they are infinitely more valid than some of our modern notions. Whenever a thing has genuine quality, it never goes out of date. Bach and Beethoven will be played and enjoyed long after "Home on the Range" has been forgotten. Bach and Beethoven have abiding quality. Shakespeare and Milton will be read as classics long after *Elmer Gentry* has been forgotten. There is a priceless ingredient called "quality" that makes the difference.

Moses was by no means an old fogey. On the contrary, he had the wit to see that some antiques are abiding and ancient moral laws cannot be ignored with impunity in this age or any other. "Thou shalt not kill," "Thou shalt not steal," "Thou shalt not commit adultery." Put them down in the middle of any era and they are relevant. "Thou shalt have no other gods before me." It does not matter whether you are talking in the United States or in Russia, you cannot trifle with that principle without paying a frightful price.

When it comes to ultimate values, "What was good enough for grandma is good enough for me." I do not care for my grandfather's horse and buggy. I prefer my Mercury. I am not interested in my grandfather's oil lamps. I prefer electricity. But I am grateful for my grandfather's love of truth. I can use that myself. I am grateful for his faith in God, a faith that carried him through difficult days in the new West and kept him steady in a rugged country. I can use my grandfather's faith in God. Indeed, I need it now perhaps more than he needed it long ago. Some things never grow old or out of date, and if your mother and father had those things, cling to them. If you think you do not need them now, just wait and be assured that you will need them.

Of course, when Moses chiseled in stone, "Honor thy father and thy mother," he assumed that the older generation had a vital faith in the Lord God of Abraham and Isaac and Jacob. He assumed parental loyalty to the moral ideals and spiritual values that flow from faith in the living God. Such faith in and loyalty to the ultimate was the testament of parents' right to respect. The commandment "Honor thy father and thy mother" breaks down and loses the force of a commandment when parents have no roots in the ultimate.

II

At the outset, then, we parents need a sense of the ultimate and the abiding as we guide our children toward maturity. However, along with that sense of the ultimate, we need capacity to distinguish between what is ultimately vital and what is not. During the Constitutional Convention somebody remarked that Benjamin Franklin had an uncanny ability to recognize the distinction between major issues and minor ones. He always kept his mind focused upon his main purpose—the stable union of the colonial people. Therefore, he never spoke to the Convention except concerning the decisive points. He could graciously surrender on unimportant issues, but he would struggle endlessly for major points. We parents need to remember that. There are ultimate, abiding standards and values we cannot ignore in our homes. When we are meeting issues on the basis of those abiding values we have the right to respect. On the other hand, there are minor matters wherein good sense invites surrender.

Some time ago I noticed an amusing cartoon, a picture of three girls in baggy jeans, shirts hanging outside. They were slouched around a record player with records scattered over the floor and overcoats flung in disarray on the chairs. A worried mother was peering anxiously around a door, obviously displeased and upset by what she saw. Her daughter, glancing over her shoulder, remarked to her two friends: "Oh, Mama is just at the awkward stage—too old to understand the way we behave and not old enough to be philosophical about it." It occurs to me that there are some things about which we shall have to be philosophical while we address ourselves to the vital.

I am altogether sure that we often annoy our children because we cannot be philosophical about things that really do not matter. If Johnny does not like orange juice, there is no use insisting that he drink it if grapefruit will do just as well. If he likes loud socks, there is no point to insisting that he ought to wear a sober blue. If he does not like the neckties you pick for him, let him pick his own. You may not like his taste, but that does not matter. Your mother thought your taste was terrible once. If he wants to wear jeans to school when you think he should wear respectable flannel trousers, why not surrender graciously? It is unimportant. It is foolish to squander authority. If you do, you are likely to win all the minor issues, and then lose one that really matters because you cannot win all the time.

I recall overhearing a conversation between two boys. They were talking about their parent problems, and one boy said to the other: "My parents are driving me nuts." Since I was an inadvertent eavesdropper, I was in no position to inquire into the boy's reason for being upset by his parents. Besides, I had been under the illusion that it was the children who usually drive their parents to distraction and not the other way about. Nevertheless, it occurred to me that the boy's feeling provided a very poor basis for obedience to the fifth commandment. Something was wrong and time would make the parent-child relationship much worse.

Often we annoy our children and make it difficult for them to honor us because we try to manage too many details of their lives. We occupy ourselves with very minor matters when we ought to be focusing upon ultimate values and issues. I felt that once when I talked with a boy who had left home because, he said, he could not stand it there any longer. What was the trouble? "Well," said he, "I'm twenty-three, and until I left home I can't remember ever making a decision for myself. Mother managed everything. She managed my clothes, she managed my friends, she managed my social life, she even decided on my career." Then, thoughtfully, he added: "I think mother usually was right, but I wanted at least the right to make a mistake."

III

Again and again I have the uncomfortable feeling that we have missed the fundamental task of parenthood. We forget too easily that it is our basic business to make ourselves unnecessary. As John the Baptist said of Jesus: "He must increase; I must decrease." Our children will honor us only if we equip them to stand on their own feet, make wise choices between alternatives and walk worthily in "the more excellent way." Issues between parents and children can be growing points, not dead-end streets. Problems have possibilities if we are trying to make ourselves unnecessary. Problems are opportunities to explore alternatives and to find the way together in mutual obedience to a will beyond our own. It is their allegiance to a will beyond their own and ours that enables our children to stand on their own feet.

It should be noted that there never was a time when it was so important for us to make ourselves unnecessary. A committee of men and women felt the problem when they met to discuss the educational needs of high school children. The first question that emerged was the problem of moral and ethical education. The problem focused around the proposed draft of eighteen-year-old boys, and the major concern was: "How can we equip our sons with capacity to make sound moral judgments when they go off to army camps?" That, believe me, is a sobering question.

Obviously the high school cannot equip our children for their task of making moral judgments, and the church alone cannot do it. It is your job and mine as parents and nobody can possibly do it for us. The business of building character adequate to bear the strain of the years begins in the crib and goes on until that day when your son or daughter goes off to stand alone. When that time comes you have no choice but to rest your right to respect on what you have said and done, what you have taught by word and by example. You will see, then, the fruit of the years.

David discovered that truth when it was too late. He loved his son Absalom deeply, and yet the cares of his kingdom were great and after all Absalom was a good boy—or was he? David really did not know. He had no time for teaching what should have been taught, no time to share the faith that had been ploughed into David's soul by fire and storm. David just hoped that maybe Absalom would come out all right. He should have known what Absalom was thinking, how little he cared for the faith of Abraham and Isaac and Jacob. When revolt came and Absalom nearly overthrew his own father, David knew how frightfully he had failed. When news came that Absalom was dead, there was agony in the heart of David: "O Absalom, my son, my son, would that I had died for thee!" But it was too late. David should have died a little year by year, died a little in giving something worthy to his son along the road.

Maybe we will learn some day that the right to respect and honor is a hard-earned right, and we never will earn it until we bend our lives to the business of making ourselves unnecessary to our children. Our children cannot possibly give obedience to the fifth commandment if they come to the need for standing alone with nothing to hold them steady. If they have no ultimates to hold them, no faith to keep them strong, no great loyalties to keep them going against the tides, why should they honor us then?

IV

That leads us to the final word, to the fact that teaching our children to stand on their own feet is far more than a matter of moral education. It is a matter of religious education. Why do you suppose Moses took four commandments to establish the priority of God before he had a word to say about ethics? Because everything he had to say about ethics had its anchors in what he said about God. That, too, is the essential truth about the Christian faith. The Beatitudes and the Sermon on the Mount presuppose the fact that God is central in life and thought. The ethic of the Christian faith is rooted and grounded in God and you cannot have the ethic without God, revealed in Jesus Christ, our Lord.

Years ago a man came to my study to say he wanted to join the church. "I thought," he said, "that I could raise my children on moral pablum, poetry and Emerson's essays. I tried the experiment, and I know now from painful experience that it won't work. I need God and so do my children." Let me add, so do you and your children, and it is sheer tragedy when that knowledge comes too late. Charles Lamb remarked facetiously on one occasion that his children "should be brought up in their father's religion, if they could find out what it was." He came to rue the day that his children never were able to find out what his religion was.

Our sense of the ultimate, our ability to distinguish between the abiding and the unimportant, and our capacity to make ourselves unnecessary to our children all depend upon our allegiance to God in Christ. Our authority as parents is a borrowed authority and it depends altogether upon an authority beyond ourselves to which we have given allegiance. H. W. Grady put the matter aptly when he wrote of Robert E. Lee that he was "royal in authority as a king and loyal to authority as a gentleman." That is our task as parents, to be "royal in authority," yet "loyal to authority," guiding and ruling not by whim or caprice, but in obedience to the authority of God.

Once, long after Moses, there came one so "royal in authority" that he spake "as one having authority and not as the scribes," but he spoke and lived as he did because he was "loyal to authority as a gentleman." Even when the shadow of death was upon him, he still was loyal to authority: "Not my will, but thine be done," he said, and marched onward toward the cross. Through all the ages since he has stood as the ethical lodestar of mankind, his love and goodness, truth and beauty anchored in the everlasting God. Across the centuries he calls to us as parents: "Follow thou me." Unless we follow, by what right shall we say to our children: "Honor thy father and thy mother."

WHEN FAITH WORKS
AT HOME

Return to thine own house, and shew how great things
God hath done unto thee.   LUKE 8:39

SUPERSTITION AND IRRATIONAL FEARS CROWDED LIFE IN THE FIRST century. Demons and angels from the spirit world fitted comfortably into the intellectual framework of the times. The neurotics and the mentally unbalanced of Jesus' day were demon possessed, and they were hopelessly lost. The Gadarene maniac was famous. He had been frightening people for years. The record says he had "had devils a long time, and wore no clothes, neither abode in any house, but in the tombs." Obviously he was a case for a psychiatrist if there had been any psychiatrists in his day.

Jesus met the Gadarene maniac quite by chance when he and the disciples beached their boat on the shore of Galilee. The maniac, who called himself "Legion," "because many devils were entered into him," was disturbed by the presence of Jesus. "I beseech thee, torment me not," he pleaded, as if the sanity and serenity of Jesus made him aware of his own mental turbulence. When Jesus spoke, commending the devils to depart from the maniac, the effect was like shock treatment, jarring the mind back to normal. In all probability the story that the devils entered into a herd of swine, driving

133

the animals into the sea, is a bit of Oriental embellishment devised to heighten the miracle. We need not be troubled by it.

What concerns us is the word of Jesus to the Gadarene when he sat before Jesus, "clothed and in his right mind." Inevitably the man expressed a desire to remain with Jesus, to preach and to teach as a disciple. Jesus had other plans for him: "Return to thine own house," he said, "and shew how great things God hath done unto thee." Quite literally Jesus said to the Gadarene, "Go home and show your nearest and dearest what God has done to you. Make clear in your own home how God has transformed you." That was no easy assignment.

I

You know as well as I do that revealing God in ourselves at home is a problem. Indeed, I suspect that our Christian spirit flounders more often at home than anywhere else. Home is a very prosaic place in many ways. If you express your Christianity working for the community chest and you do a good job, you get at least honorable mention. If you share helpfully in the work in the church, you get credit for what you do. But at home there is not much of a cheering section. You can do without what you want, sacrifice for your children, wait on your children and do for them endlessly, and it is just taken for granted. The time comes when you are "fed up" and you need God to save you from resentment and self-pity.

When you stop to think about the matter, it is clear you are not at your best at home. In public you put your best foot forward. You are the soul of graciousness, on your best behavior. You dress your best and act your best. You make a good impression and people are grateful for your fine spirit. At a meeting you are conciliatory and diplomatic and unselfish. You are respected and admired in your club, where you do more than your share of the work. People who know you say you are "a grand person," and you really are. Then you go home, a bit fagged, your energy depleted. There is work to be done and nobody but you to do it. Somebody has to get the dinner and clean up the kitchen afterward. Nobody thinks to tell you that you are "a grand person," and when you get into a house dress and apron, you do not feel very grand. Quite possibly your graciousness slips and your charm loses its luster. At such a time it is not easy to demonstrate what God has done for you.

In business a man is either the boss or else he is a subordinate. If he is the boss, he has a certain standard of dignity and decorum and diplomacy to maintain. If he wants efficiency and loyalty he has to be at least a reasonably likable and dependable person. On the other hand, if he is a subordinate, his disposition is conditioned by his desire to hold his job or get a promotion. He keeps his temper under control of necessity and he endures annoyances for the sake of his job. On the whole he appears at his best most of the time. When he comes home, things are different. Being boss at the office does not automatically confer the right to be boss at home, neither does it insure the capacity for dignity, decorum and diplomacy at home. Being a subordinate at the office by no means insures that a man will be a subordinate at home. Quite the contrary is likely to be the case. Besides, both the boss and the subordinate come home having given their best energies to their jobs. They are likely to be somewhat wilted by the time they hang their hats in the closet and head for the easy chair. It is something of a strain at that point to be confronted with the problem of Willie's poor report card or Susie's misbehavior at school. Such a time provides a glorious opportunity to demonstrate what God has done for you.

It should be noted, too, that children seldom appear at their best at home. When they are invited for a week end with a neighbor, they usually amaze the neighbor. Their behavior is exemplary. They are the soul of courtesy and consideration. The parents of their friends wonder how you have trained them so well. You wonder, too, because when they come home they act like young Indians.

Their table manners are atrocious and their behavior is impossible. Children are precisely like the rest of us. They let down at home. They are under discipline at school most of the day, then they wear themselves out playing. They come home a little jaded. God has not had long enough to demonstrate what He can do with them.

II

"Return to thine own house, and shew how great things God hath done unto thee." It is about as difficult a commandment as Jesus ever uttered, but it also is one of the most important. Homecoming is a time for selfless consideration of those we love. But have you ever noticed that homecoming after a hard day's work or a busy time shopping is likely to be a time when you are preoccupied with yourself? In any case, you are not in the mood to be either sympathetic or understanding when you meet the other members of the family. On the contrary, your defenses are up, prepared to resist the impact of family problems if you are able to manage it.

Actually, however, the time you spend coming home from wherever you have been needs to be a time of preparation for understanding. While you are walking home from the elevated station, or into the house from the garage, give God a chance to get you under control. Just a bit of scripture repeated under the breath may help: "Be still, and know that I am God!" "Peace I leave with you, my peace I give unto you." It does not take much to remind you that the world does not center in you. It does not take much to remind you you are supposed to "return to thine own house, and shew how great things God hath done unto thee."

Sometimes I have been amazed to discover how quickly God can change my mood when I give Him a chance. The trouble is that we forget to give God a chance, and we blunder home in an ominous mood and of course ominous things happen. Oren Arnold describes the time he came home from his office at the end of a brutal day. He was in a grim mood and almost before he got his coat off he was berating the children for nothing that mattered in the least. A little while later he heard his thirteen-year-old daughter saying to his eight-year-old, "Daddy's off the beam tonight. He didn't mean it." And the eight-year-old replied: "Yea, I know."

Often I have the feeling that we ask our children to understand too much because we understand too little. We come home "off the beam" and we think everybody else in the family is "off the beam." It works that way, you know, and it really is not funny in the least. We need to come home with understanding hearts and minds nourished on our fellowship with God. There is no use in making excuses for ourselves. Excuses will not help in the least when the family has floundered into a state of explosive anger because somebody got "off the beam." Excuses can't change things; God can.

In his delightful book, *Ideas Have Legs,* Peter Howard describes how he would come home from work with a chip on his shoulder, exasperated by the strain of newspaper work on London's Fleet Street. In no time at all he would have the family upset and everybody spoiling for a fight. "I would fight for my own way, regardless," he wrote. I would "slam the door and shut it on all negotiation." Then something happened to Peter Howard. He got religion and it worked at home and everywhere else. When he got himself "on the beam" the whole family got "on the beam." Instead of coming home with a chip on his shoulder he began to come home with an understanding heart. He says very bluntly that God did for him what he could not do for himself. Quite literally, he returned to his house day after day to show "how great things" God had done for him. His wife and his children scarcely knew him!

That can happen in your home despite all the strains and pressures you meet in the world day after day. Just give God a chance somewhere along the way home. Stop long enough to say just a hint of a prayer. "O God, give me grace to understand and to bring a bit of joy to my home." You don't need a closet or even a chapel; a side street or your car can be your prayer closet and your prayer closet will pay off with more peace and love than you have known at home for many a long year. Don't miss your chance to make faith work at home. Don't go blundering and fumbling your chance to make home what it ought to be. "Return to thine own house, and shew what great things God hath done unto thee."

III

Somehow we have come by the notion that we have to do important things for God. Maybe if we could preach like the preacher or run the church like the elders and the trustees, or build libraries and hospitals like millionaires, that would be important. The Gadarene had some such notion. After he had come to himself he wanted to travel with Jesus, preaching like the disciples. Jesus, however, had another idea of what was important: "Return to thine own house," he said, as if the really important things were done at home.

It appears strange, I know, but God seems to work in out-of-the-way corners. He does not concern Himself much with what you think is important. He has other ideas. His future rarely springs out of grand occasions proclaimed in newspaper headlines; it works its way up softly through common things, out of dark crannies, by way of the casual word a man speaks to his son or his wife. The things that really make the future are done in the shadows, where no eyes are even aware of them. There in the shadows things are happening that will fix the destinies of a hundred years to come. Behind the doors that have swung open for you day after day important things are really happening.

Probably you will not be sent out under the will of God to do startling or impossible things. You are quite likely ordained to do quiet, unspectacular things. There was nothing spectacular about Abraham Lincoln's mother; at least nobody in her own generation noticed her talents. She was a good homemaker, under very great difficulties, and she was a wise mother, but what she did was done in the shadows where nobody noticed much. Joseph was just a carpenter in an obscure little village in Palestine. It never occurred to him when he made "easy yokes" that fitted properly that he was fashioning the future. But Jesus watched him at his toil and sensed the worth of fine workmanship. When Joseph made good doors that swung easily on their hinges he did not suspect that he was opening doors to a better future. Nevertheless, "easy yokes" and open doors are symbols now of the life that is life indeed.

Important things happen at home, in the shadows where nobody sees. To be sure, the impact is felt in the world. The genius of Louisa May Alcott made a mark on the world, but the really important things happened around the dinner table in the house of Amos Bronson Alcott. Henry Ward Beecher and Harriet Beecher Stowe made profound marks upon the America of their day, but the really important things happened in the home of Lyman Beecher, where Harriet and Henry got their start. Behind every great sermon that ever is preached is a spirit at home that made it possible. Behind every great book that is written is a fellowship and a spirit at home that inspired it. Back of every successful business adventure is a quality of life at home that sustained it. The really decisive things in life occur in the shadows at home where nobody notices what goes on.

God's Kingdom is not built by experts who make blueprints for the good society. It is built in the shadows where ordinary folk create character, where life rubs against life. A preacher friend of mine had a letter once from a parishioner of a former parish, who wrote: "We are grateful you were here because some of you rubbed off on us." Well, some of us rubs off on our children, and our children rub off on other children, and what we are rubs off on those around us. The quality of life we are creating at home rubs off on the world to make the world better or worse, richer or poorer. That is really important.

That is what Paul had in mind when he wrote to "the saints in Caesar's household." They were obscure folk, servants and slaves in the imperial household, and Paul wrote to them: "Be kindly affectioned one to another . . . ; not slothful in business; fervent in spirit; serving the Lord; rejoicing in hope; patient in tribulation; continuing instant in prayer; distributing to the necessity of saints; given to hospitality." Puny things, don't you think? Why waste time writing a letter about such unimportant matters? "Affectionate," "given to hospitality." And those to whom Paul wrote were slaves, mostly, pitted against the mailed fist of the Roman Empire. But by the Grace of God some of what they were "rubbed off." What happened in obscure corners in Caesar's household, in the catacombs of Rome, in unnoticed homes in the imperial city was of decisive importance.

No wonder Jesus sent the Gadarene back to his home, to the obscure, unnoticed shadows where history is made. He understood more clearly than anybody before him or since that the simple, unimportant things that happen in homes like yours and mine are the really important things. Don't let anybody tell you that in a world like this, hanging on the edge of an abyss, the homely, Christian virtues flowing from ordinary homes can make no difference in history. That is the devil's device to wreck the stuff of which God is making His future. "Return to thine own house, and shew what great things God hath done unto thee."

YOUR NEIGHBOR'S HOME
AND YOURS

❦

Thou shalt not commit adultery.   EXODUS 20:14

❦

WILL DURANT, WHO IS NOT WHAT YOU WOULD CALL AN ORTHODOX Christian, laments the fact that infidelity in marriage is increasing because God has become little more than a popular superstition in modern life. Moses would not be surprised by that observation. He knew full well that faith and morals are intimately interlinked. Therefore, he instituted the moral rearmament of the Children of Israel by a vigorous affirmation of the sovereignty of God. After he had placed God at the center of things in the first four commandments, he got around to the ethical consequences of faith in the God of Abraham and Isaac and Jacob. Knowing that man is worth something to God, Moses chiseled in stone: "Thou shalt not kill." Then he turned his attention to the sanctity of marriage with the blunt words: "Thou shalt not commit adultery."

It is significant to notice that the seventh commandment is a corollary to the sixth. If human personality is sacred, we have no business trifling with human affections. If human personality counts supremely in the economy of God, we have no right to tangle it in conflicts or debase it with consciousness of guilt. If character is the crowning goal of living and the source of meaning in our lives, we thwart the very will of God by any act of ours that undercuts the goal. As Moses saw the matter, marriage is a means by which we reach the moral and spiritual ends of life. It is a means to endless growth in all that makes a full-orbed soul. "Thou shalt not commit adultery," and stunt the self God meant to be.

I

When we look at marriage discerningly we see it as an adventure in which a man and a woman surrender their separateness on the altar of creative togetherness. "Forsaking all others," each trusts life to the other "until death do us part." To be sure, at the beginning their togetherness is a tenuous thing, a possibility, not a fact. They bring their separateness to the altar—their opinions, their separate wills, their inherited characteristics—and the elements of separateness endure sometimes too long. Self-will is slow to bend and tensions mount that thwart togetherness. The self is stubborn, yielding with reluctance to a harness. It moves by fits and starts, often pulling off the road and spilling romance in the ditch.

There is a bit of truth in the ancient Hindu story of creation, recording how God created woman to share a common life with man. He took the beauty of the flowers, the song of the birds, the colors of the rainbow, the kiss of the breeze, the laughter of the waves and the gentleness of the lamb, wove them into a woman and gave her to Adam for a wife. The Hindu Adam was happy, and he and his wife roamed about the beautiful earth. But after a while Adam came to God and said, "Take this woman away from me, for I cannot live with her." And God listened to the request and took her away. Then Adam became lonely and unhappy, so in due time he came to God and said: "Give me back my wife, for I cannot live without her." In his infinite wisdom, God gave Eve back to Adam. But again, after a few days, Adam came to God saying: "Please take back this Eve that Thou hast created, for I swear I cannot live with her." Again God consented. When finally

Adam came a fourth time and complained he could not live without Eve, God made him promise that he would not change his mind again and that he would throw in his lot with her for better or for worse.

Life has not changed much since then, and the Hindu Adam and Eve are ourselves with pressures pulling us apart and yet drawing us together once again. And yet, if love is honest and our minds at least in part mature, we grow together more and more under the discipline of the years. Each year we live together the things we have in common multiply, the joys and sorrows, the triumphs and the failures. Increasingly our memories embrace a common store of experience and the fibers that bind us together become stronger. Slowly we learn to understand each other, the moods that sweep like storms across the days, the weariness that weighs us down, the ancient half-forgotten hurts that fester now and then. Our minds tune in to the same station and we hear the same music together.

T. S. Eliot sensed the truth when he made Peter say in *The Cocktail Party,*

It is not her interest in me that I miss—
But these moments in which we seemed to share some perception,
Some feeling, some indefinable experience
In which we were both unaware of ourselves.[1]

The moments of shared perception when we are unaware of ourselves may come when we are painting the front porch or making gardens together, or perhaps when we are sitting side by side in church or quietly beside a glowing hearth fire. It is important to notice, however, that the togetherness of such moments is the consequence of something we share. We look outward together toward the same point of reference and in a curious alchemy of the spirit lose sight of ourselves.

There is a striking sentence in the marriage ceremony that sug-

[1] *The Cocktail Party,* by T. S. Eliot, Harcourt Brace & Company, N. Y., 1950. Used by permission.

gests the focal point of all togetherness. Both the bride and the groom promise to "encourage each other in things that pertain to God." That is no sentimental promise, but an invitation to shared perception, a summons to find a meeting point for minds that is above the petty things that preserve our separateness. Indeed, the whole concept of Christian marriage has its focus in the conviction that marriage is more than a contract between two people. It is a covenant between a man and a woman and God, wherein two people achieve togetherness asking not "What do I want?" but rather "What does God want?" When two minds meet in the question, "What does God want?" the shared perception of a worthy Will beyond their own is the testament of togetherness. Love is far more than a horizontal affair wherein two people look across the breakfast table at each other. It is a perpendicular affair, wherein two people look upward together toward God in Christ.

When we share a common perception of God and His will for us, we find a growing wonder and beauty in our togetherness, and we grow richer with the passing years. Indeed, the crowning glory of life is the sublime togetherness of a man and a woman traveling through the sunset years hand in hand, approaching the end of the road more deeply in love than when they stood before the altar to link their lives for the adventure. Surely, only a fool would spoil the possibility of such togetherness and sweep away the chance of a man and a woman for a growing life together. "Thou shalt not commit adultery."

II

Marriage is not only an adventure in togetherness, it is also a pilgrimage in which two people link their lives for mutual support and strength, "for better, for worse; for richer, for poorer." Together a man and a woman can meet temptations and tempests that would break them if they stood alone. Together they can manage disappointment and failure, sorrow and heartache. Alone? Ah, God was wise when "He set the solitary in families." Bound together in homes where faith and trust abide, the storms cannot break us. The world may rage with tumult and shouting outside, but if the hearth is warm inside we can meet the tumult with a steady strength.

We need the strength of love to hold us steady in more ways than one. The world defies the best we know and invites our failure to fulfill the claims of the highest. Somebody with a bit of wry wit noted that whether he read a magazine or went to a movie it was "sex of one and sex of the other." Judging by modern advertising copy sex sells anything—soap, automobiles, tobacco or Mack Trucks —indiscriminately. In due time, I suppose, Carnation Milk's contented cows will be wearing bathing suits! Modern novelists, with an eye on sales, have effectively destroyed the sanctity of sex, and pulp magazines are shoddy beyond measure.

Against the tides of license in our world today we need the strength of our togetherness. We need what my father had years ago when he traveled week by week, a young man, in the mining camps of Colorado. We were talking once about the things that tempt a man and leave him poorer than he might have been. How did he manage through the days to be loyal to the best that he knew? His answer was a simple one: "I loved your mother, Son. She kept me steady." And so it ought to be. Hosea wrote of the "bands of love" that fling the "everlasting arms" of God around two people journeying together. He says God held him with "bands of love," and so it always is, for the love that binds a man and a woman in a great togetherness is but one aspect of the love of God that holds us all.

Linked together by the love of God that binds us to each other, our strength to bear the strain and stress of life is multiplied. Thomas Carlyle might have been a hack writer, long since forgotten, save for his wife Jane. Through days of defeat and failure she was his source of strength to carry on. Years after Jane was gone,

Thomas wrote: "She was the sunshine of my poor, dripping days." So it was, and so it can be for us all. Some years ago a woman voiced the truth when she said as she stood at the grave of her husband: "Through the years he was like a sturdy tree on which I leaned."

A man and a woman, standing together, loving each other, are more than the sum of their separateness. There is a "plus," a strength beyond their own that is a gift of grace. Did you see the Associated Press photograph of a Korean man and his wife, weighted down with their possessions, plodding along a shell-pocked road hand in hand? Ah, believe me, she was more than herself, and he was more than himself as they faced the worst that life could do with their togetherness. "Marching along together," nothing could destroy their spirit or their hope; nothing could keep them from going on. Even on that tragic road, homeless refugees, they were not helpless.

When two people link their lives in a great togetherness for mutual support and strength they find the strength of God. Do you want to spoil the possibility of that? "Thou shalt not commit adultery."

III

Marriage is not only an adventure in togetherness, and a pilgrimage in which two people link their lives for mutual support; it is also a long journey in the course of which a man and a woman achieve life's richest values. They find their lives by losing their separateness. They fulfill themselves in self-surrender. They win their deepest joy not in pleasing themselves but in pleasing each other. Robert Browning felt the truth when he wrote to Elizabeth Barrett, his wife:

> I would I could adopt your will,
> See with your eyes, and set my heart
> Beating by yours, and drink my fill

At your soul's springs—your part my part
In life, for good or ill.

To will each other's will in mutual self-surrender is the crowning
evidence of togetherness, the final glory of our lives together.

To be sure, it takes bigness of mind and spirit, it takes maturity
to reach the end that is so far away at the beginning. There is no
easy road across the years to unity of being and thinking. It takes
endless patience and fidelity; it takes steadfastness and loyalty
through years of adjustment, but the goal is worth the dusty road
we travel. Who wants to be free who has found fulfillment and
peace in togetherness? Who wants to roam highways and byways
who has found a narrow road that leads to happiness and joy?

Bertrand Russell, philosopher and social historian, once took the
view that old-fashioned marriage was outmoded. He insisted that
fulfillment came in freedom, not in fetters. He announced his views
in a book called *Marriage and Morals,* which was a popular procla-
mation of independence from outworn moral customs. He announced that sex was a matter of convenience and disposition.
What he said sounded plausible enough, but its cutting edge was
somewhat dulled by the fact that Mr. Russell tried out his own
philosophy and found it sadly wanting. He and his wife decided
to go modern in a large way. They would not be inhibited by the
silly inhibitions of an outworn religion. They would please themselves. So, they agreed between them to ignore the seventh commandment if it suited their fancy. They were broad-minded enough
to accept the facts of nature and enjoy life on their own terms. Life
would be wonderful without the onerous demands of fidelity. Being
both a philosopher and a historian, Mr. Russell should have known
that marriage could not be wonderful on his own terms. His experiment ended in divorce and recrimination. He learned the hard way
what Moses could have told him long centuries ago.

We do not achieve life's richest values simply by trying to please
ourselves. Time without end, we please ourselves and find we are

not pleased! We have our own way only to discover we did not really want our way when we got it. We battle stupidly for our point of view, only to learn in sad experience that it was not God's point of view. We fight for freedom to go our own course, and then discover that our freedom bores us terribly. Some day we will learn that the deepest treasures of human experience are won from self-surrender for the sake of togetherness. We will learn, or we will die in frustration feeling that life, and marriage too, are a "tale told by an idiot."

The prodigal son set out to please himself. The "far country" seemed alluring. With unfettered abandon he "devoured his substance in riotous living." He pleased himself all right. He got what he wanted; had his fill of everything he wanted, but it turned out to be only a husk with no substance at all. Loyalty and honor, faith and integrity, truth and beauty were the substance of the life he really wanted. In the end he had to turn back and start over when he "came to himself." Until he turned back he was growing poorer, devoid of values life can use to build the substance of the soul. Before he was done he knew that pleasing himself was a shabby business.

The deepest treasures of the human spirit are not won on selfish roads. They grow from a togetherness that somehow loses sight of self. Character is fashioned and honesty is nourished along the road we journey together. Loyalty and forgiveness enhance our stature along the trail we walk together. Patience and steadfastness enrich our souls when we march across the years hand in hand. By what strange perversion of the mind would anyone destroy another's chance to win from life the noblest treasures that it holds? "Thou shalt not commit adultery."

IV

There is one thing more we need to note. When all else has been said, we need to see that marriage is a long road two people travel to God. If "God is love" as we believe He is, then God is in the love we bear each other in our homes. Where love is growing, our experience of God is growing. Wherever love is turning into a great togetherness, God is coming closer than He ever was before. When children come, and love has found another link to hold it and to expand its sweep, God is very close.

We may be blind—we often are—like Jacob when he said, "Surely God was in this place, and I knew it not." But if we have the wit to see Him in our love and trust and to acknowledge He "was in the beginning" of our love, "is now and ever shall be," we win a benediction and a crown. Whoever would be cheap enough to spoil a thing that God Himself has wrought? "Thou shalt not commit adultery."

BETWEEN THE GENERATIONS

Children, obey your parents. . . . And, ye fathers, provoke not your children to wrath.　　EPHESIANS 6:1–4

THE APOSTLE PAUL WAS A FAIR-MINDED MAN AND SURPRISINGLY DIS-
cerning when he wrote concerning family life. In his letter to
the Ephesians he says bluntly to the rising generation, "Children,
obey your parents"; do what you are told to do and don't argue
about it. Then, as if he understood the unreasonableness of parents,
he went on to say, "Ye fathers, provoke not your children unto
wrath." With one hand Paul put the children in their place and
with the other he neatly polished off the parents. He was well aware
that conflict between the generations was a matter for which youth
and age were jointly responsible. Indeed, he has quite as much to
say to prodigal parents as to prodigal children on the theory there
are as many of one as of the other.

When I stop long enough to try to see myself as my children see
me at home I am quite sure Paul's admonition to fathers was in
order. Our children must find us parents quite inexplicable at times.
I suspect we appear an irritating, provoking necessity. When it
comes to the evening newspaper I suppose I seem a bit like a Flying
Fortress on a vengeance mission. My children are quite unable to
understand why a mere newspaper should be sacred, or why I

should object if I find it scattered over the living-room floor. There are times when my sons must think I have joined the Gestapo—especially at bedtime. It is quite beyond them to comprehend why getting into bed five minutes or fifteen minutes after the appointed bedtime hour should be a matter of decisive importance. Then, too, so far as the boys can see, there is no good reason for getting irritated because the hammer, saw and automatic screw driver are left out in the rain. What is a little rust among friends?

Of course, the difficulty is in the fact that the generations look at life from opposite directions. When you think of the contradictions which have to be resolved within the average family it is a wonder our homes do not fall apart like an overloaded Toonerville Trolley. There is a suggestion of the difference between the points of view of parents and their children in a cartoon I once clipped from the evening paper. Willie quite evidently has torn his trousers sliding into home base, and for his carelessness he is in the process of being spanked by his very irate father. Between spanks Willie is saying with injured dignity, "The whole neighborhood is cheering my home run, and this is the appreciation I get at home." Being a hero or a villain depends entirely upon the point of view.

Take almost any area of thinking you please and you will find youth and age, children and parents looking at life from opposite poles. Age, quite naturally, is conservative, resistant to change in the order of things as they are. Age is forever saying, "Stop rocking the boat"; but youth would rather rock the boat than sit still, which, of course, explains why revolutionists from the Maccabees to Mussolini appeal to youth. Besides, the older we grow, the less energy we parents have; but our children possess boundless vigor which they spend with lavish enthusiasm. They wear us down until we wonder how much longer we can take it without nervous collapse.

Then, too, age looks backward; youth looks forward. Age has too many memories; youth has too few. Age has too little time ahead; youth has too little time behind. There is a hint of the difference in points of view in the conversation of a father and his son as they paused in the midst of a mountain climb. The father, on the portly, puffing side of forty, looked back toward the valley below and said: "Son, just look how far we have come." And the boy, looking toward the snow-capped peak ahead, replied, "I know, Dad, but just look where we are going." Youth has no way of knowing how much hardship and heartbreak lie on the way to the snow-capped peak ahead; age, long on the rugged road, cannot forget how hardly even a little elevation is won.

I might go on describing the differences between the generations, with youth endlessly optimistic, age likely to be pessimistic; youth noisy and exuberant, while age is quiet; youth playful, age mostly played out; youth extravagant with money, age cautious and saving of resources. But the truth is clear: there is a vast chasm to be bridged between the generations, a chasm whose focus is in the home, where the generations meet.

When we parents face the contradictions we meet in our children, it is quite natural for us to seize upon the first half of Paul's admonition: "Children, obey your parents." We forget all too easily that our right to obedience is contingent upon the wisdom of our demands. We assume, quite without warrant, that parenthood automatically confers the right to demand obedience from our children. The fact of the matter was suggested by a wise minister who once shared in the installation of a younger contemporary. Said he at the conclusion of his prayer: "Grant that this congregation may yield obedience to its chosen leader so long as he is obedient to Christ. Amen."

Believe me, that is a sobering prayer not only for a minister, but also for a parent, because it suggests the right to obedience is conditioned by our own obedience to a law more cogent than our whims. Indeed, that idea is implicit in all democracy, for the distinguishing feature of the democratic way is that we are governed by law and not by the unfettered wills of men. We yield obedience to our leaders only when they in turn are obedient to the laws of the land. Their right to demand co-operation of us is contingent upon their loyalty to the laws they are sworn to uphold.

After the same fashion, we parents who demand obedience from our children are faced with the necessity of squaring our demands with the "mind of Christ." Not petulance but principle undergirds our authority. Not power, but dedication to abiding precept gives us the right to command. What stirs our children to wrath is the unreasoned demand, the petulant order, the obstinate refusal. Our difficulty lies in the fact that it is so much easier to command than to offer sound reasons for what we command. It is much simpler to compel obedience from little children in spite of their wrath than to exercise the patience of sweet reasonableness. It is less trouble to carry a small boy upstairs to bed kicking and yelling than to win his cooperation through ingenuity, patience and explanation. Unhappily, unreasoned discipline and angry coercion yield an inevitable crop of rebellion when childhood turns to adolescence. Thus we are confronted with the necessity of resolving the contradictions between parents and children creatively or they will resolve themselves disastrously. Together, in creative explanation, we may arrive at mutual respect for abiding principles.

That brings me to the question that is basic to parenthood. What are we trying to accomplish? What do we wish to achieve by way of discipline? The danger is suggested in the frank and passionate letter of John Ruskin to his father. "You thwarted me," he says, "in all the earnest fire and passion of my life." The truth is that the business of parenthood is the training of children to bear the weight of future independence. So,

> I shall not fling
> My strong, my deadly noose of years
> About the neck of youth,
> Nor with my flagging life and graying hairs
> Tether him from his choice.
> But, smiling, I shall free him,
> Remembering anew

The swift, keen whir of hope,
The tensing muscle, the ecstatic breath
With which, long, long ago
I leapt into my race.
And though he run an alien course,
I shall not call him back,—
I shall rejoice.

If only we are wise enough to see that we are training our children for independence, preparing them to think for themselves, decide for themselves, and stand on their own feet. The lion and the wolf teach their cubs to hunt and to fend for themselves in forest and field. The bird painfully pushes the fledgling from the nest in what seems a cruel demand that the infant bird win its wings and achieve independence. We parents are different. We cling to the unfortunate illusion that we are perpetually "indispensable," when in reality we are "expendable." We are flattered by the feeling that our children still are dependent upon us, even though they may have children of their own. We are a little hurt if our children strike out completely on their own.

If in our homes, where the generations meet, we have been wise, creating mutual respect for abiding principles, inspiring ideals, building spiritual fellowships into the lives of our children, we shall rejoice in their independence even though they run "an alien course." We shall fear their independence only if we have failed in our homes to lay the foundations for their freedom. If the bases of liberty have been laid, we shall be able to trust that our children will find their way in the end, even though they wander uncertainly for a while.

There is a delightful episode recorded in the life of Phillips Brooks, one of the great preachers of his day. Like most young people at some time or another, he declared his religious independence of his parents. Home from college for vacation, he went into the kitchen one day and announced with pontifical finality, "Mother, I do not believe in God." His mother, quite unperturbed, continued mixing pie crust. Somewhat disturbed by his failure to get a rise, young Brooks repeated, "Mother, I have decided that I cannot believe in God." Mrs. Brooks smiled indulgently and replied, "Very well, Phil, your mother does." That was all. It was enough. The foundations had been laid, and Mrs. Brooks had no fear of her son's independence. He would grow wiser by and by.

The secret of such parental security in the independence of children is to be found in the quality of their shared and transmitted loyalties. The truth is suggested strikingly in the life of Daniel Webster. His life, says his biographer, "presents a model of consistency. Love of the union was his earliest allgiance," and it was his last as well. The ideals constantly held before Daniel Webster as a boy were Washington and the Constitution. Ebenezer Webster, his father, was outwardly a plain New England farmer, not particularly different from thousands of others in that New Hampshire country where he had set up his home. He was rough mannered, unschooled, hard working, of deep religious faith, patriotic in primitive, fervid fashion; and his soul similarly burned with zeal for Washington and the Constitution. Both these enthusiasms he had acquired by authentic experience. Ebenezer had been one of the first of those minutemen who were roused to enlistment on the eve of Bunker Hill; he had fought at the siege of Boston, at Long Island and at White Plains, as well as in most of the campaigns of the Revolution, finally reaching colonel's rank. More important were his several meetings with Washington, which he loved to describe to the admiring Daniel. At West Point, on the eve of Arnold's treason, Ebenezer was selected by Washington as officer of the guard, and Washington's commendation on that occasion was one of Daniel's finest inheritances. "Captain Webster," said Washington, "I am sure I can trust you."

Well, throughout all the turbulence of his life Daniel Webster was guided by his loyalty to the Union for which his father and his hero fought. He could be trusted to stand for Union when Civil War threatened; he could be trusted to use his eloquence and his influence for Union no matter what it cost. He could be trusted with his own independence because his liberty rested upon a magnificent loyalty.

Paul feels the compulsion of a similarly significant loyalty when he says: "The love of Christ constraineth us." Loving his Lord, Paul could be trusted to stand by the good, the true and the just; loving his Master, Paul could be trusted to keep faith with himself. His life was channeled through a strait gate and along a narrow way not by coercion, but by the constraint of an enriching loyalty. So, Paul warned parents against inviting the wrath of their children by way of unreasoned coercion, advising them instead to "nurture" their children "in the admonition of the Lord."

There is deep insight in what Paul wrote his friends at Ephesus. He understood that how we choose between alternatives, how we use our independence depends upon the loyalties that lead us. It has been the tragedy of our generation that the younger generation, bereft of great spiritual dedications, has embraced treacherous temporal affections. Both Hitler and Mussolini were material substitutes for spiritual dedications. Communism, with its ritual, its faith and its Karl Marx, is a temporal equivalent of a spiritual imperative. Men must love and belong to something. Lacking the living Christ, they are fair game for tyrants with a flair for dramatics. Without dedications giving direction to their lives, they are easy victims for any "wind of doctrine" blowing their way.

James has a word for our need when he speaks of "the royal law" of liberty in love. It is the only liberty that is safe and the only independence secure in the face of temptation. It is liberty guided by love for one who stood sun-crowned above the storms of his day and hurled his life against the evils of his time in eternal defense of the truth that makes men free. We shall rejoice in the independence of our children when we know they have been "nurtured" in the love of Christ; when we know that in our homes, where the generations meet, they have heard the call, "Follow me."

Random

❯❯❯❯❯❯❯❯

The soul of man is like the rolling world,
One half in day, the other dipped in night;
The one has music and the flying cloud,
The other, silence and the wakeful stars.

Alexander Smith, "Horton"

THE UNTOLD STORY
OF JUDAS

> And Judas Iscariot, he that was one of the twelve, went away unto the chief priests, that he might deliver him unto them.　　　　　　　　　　　　　MARK 14:10

JUDAS ALWAYS HAS BEEN SOMETHING OF AN ENIGMA TO CHRISTIANS. How could this strange man, the friend and companion of Jesus, betray his Lord and Master for thirty pieces of silver? Through the years I have wondered about Judas. What lay behind his betrayal of Jesus? Was he merely seduced by silver, a victim of inordinate greed? Was he led astray by some mysterious mental twist? Or, was he the victim of a misguided dream of worldly power?

We know little of the early life of this man, save that he was the son of Simon of Kerioth, a potter, and himself a molder and worker in clay. Simon was a Zealot, whose hatred of the Romans knew no bounds. When his own life had reached the hour of "the destruction that wasteth at noonday," one hope still burned in his heart. Judas, his son, must be "a man of God; sturdy of limb and perfect in the law," a hero of Israel like his great namesake, Judas Maccabeus.

Inheriting the spirit of his father, and chafing under the yoke of Roman oppression, Judas longed for a Messiah who would destroy

Rome and establish God's Kingdom on earth. That hope motivated his life and went far to make him what he was.

I now want Judas to tell his own story as he might have told it to his sister a few hours after his betrayal of Jesus. The story has been gleaned from the gospels and other scholarly sources. Much of the narrative has been supplied by my own imagination which I think has been faithful to the facts. It is thus that Judas speaks:

There is a frightful tempest in my soul, Mary. I see too late what I have done. I have betrayed the son of God. I hate, I loathe the deed I have done. Why did I do it? God only knows. Perhaps because I was too blind to see the truth. A king he was, I am sure; but not the kind of king I had dreamed about. I thought Messiah was to be a soldier, not a servant. I expected him to rule the world by the might of the sword and not by love. If he had been a soldier, I would have died for him gladly. Hate burned in my soul: not love such as his. I sought revenge. I could not forgive. It was bitterness that drove me on.

How could it be otherwise, my sister? All my life I have dreamed of fighting beside a mighty Messiah. That was my father's dream before me. It has been the hope of Israel since the days of the kings. Did not John the Baptist say a mighty one would come to redeem Israel? My heart was stirred when I heard John proclaim the coming of Messiah. After John had spoken, I was baptized in the River Jordan that I might be pure enough to serve Him well. I came away prepared to follow my Messiah wherever He should lead.

Then came Jesus. John knew him when he came and told me he was the one whom God had sent. When I saw his face and heard his voice, I knew he had come from God. He was strong and handsome, clean and fine, a soldier, every inch of him. I shall never forget the day he spoke to me with words that pierced me through: "Come thou after me, Judas, thou molder and maker of vases and jars, and I will make you a molder and maker of men." God knows

I would have trained his men. I would have made them soldiers, molded them as hard as iron and as steady as the stars.

Peter and James and John and Jude, they all felt just as I. They were eager for the coming fray. And when we saw his power, how he stilled the waves, healed the sick, caused the blind to see and held the multitudes entranced, we knew he was the one to save Israel from her foes and bring the sword of God to crush our tyrants and break the necks of evil kings.

Then we all went sick. He threw away a chance to make himself the king. Herod cut off the head of John and served it on a platter for his unholy queen. The fury of the people knew no bounds. They rushed to Jesus as the one of all able to answer the outrage and competent to crush our foes. But he sent the crowds away telling them that they who took the sword would die by the sword. He bade us love our enemies and bless the ones who persecuted us. Those were strange words for Messiah to speak, but I did not give up hope.

At the synagogue he offended the priests with strange sayings: "Ye worship ye know not what," he said. "Not one of you hath found God in his heart. Ye have taken your God from your books. Ye think to win God's favor by prayers and sacrifices, when he asks only justice, love and truth. Ye think the synagogues and the temple alone are holy. Foolish men. The hour cometh and now is when true worshippers shall worship in spirit and in truth. The whole earth is his temple. In the thunder ye shall hear the voice of his strength; go ye out beneath the stars and ye shall feel his peace.

"Take of his strength and his peace, and build in your midst the Kingdom of Heaven. For the Kingdom cometh not with observation; neither shall they say, lo here, or lo there, for behold, the Kingdom of God is within you."

The Pharisees murmured against him and made plans to destroy him. But he was afraid of nothing. He faced the priests as if they had no power to harm him. I think he would have defied Caesar himself without fear of danger or of death.

When the multitudes came to him in Capernaum, eager for stirring words and crying for a sign from heaven, he talked instead of everlasting life and refused them any sign. "My kingdom," he said, "is not of this world." That day there were many who turned sadly away and "walked with him no more." When he saw them going, he turned to us with a question in his eyes. "Will you go too?" he asked.

I knew not what to say. I was heartsick at what he had done. Popular leaders, I knew, must tell the people what they want to hear. But he said hard things. He talked more of crosses than of crowns. He spoke more of suffering than of conquest. He preached love and kindness, when hate and bitterness were in the hearts of men. I did not understand but I think Peter caught a glimpse of what I now have learned. He answered for us all, "No, Master, we will not go. To whom can we go? Thou hast the words of eternal life."

My task was growing more and more difficult. I had been elected treasurer of the group to raise money to support our band and to feed the poor. That was an easy task when people thought Jesus had come to set them free from Rome. But when he repulsed all efforts to make him king; when he spoke of love and peace, not war and strife, the people would not give to sustain our labors.

Besides, the scribes and Pharisees were stirring up the people against him. They were jealous of his power. He said that love was greater than their laws. They caused an awful tempest when he took the coin they offered and admonished them to "render unto Caesar the things that are Caesar's." They scarcely heard the rest of what he said. They heard enough, for surely no Messiah would speak thus in defense of Rome.

Then came the worst of all. One day he told us sadly, "I must go up to Jerusalem and be rejected by the elders and chief priests and scribes, and be killed." A Messiah murdered? Impossible. It could not be. I spoke to Peter and he was as anxious as I. He went to Jesus to protest, to turn the Master's face from Jerusalem. He need not go there where his enemies were so strong. Why should he risk his life needlessly? But Jesus turned upon his friend with quiet eyes and said sternly, "Get thee behind me, Satan." It was as if he thought Peter an emissary of Satan rather than a friend bidding him to save his life.

I was near my wit's end, my anger against him rising day by day. All Israel was disappointed in him, and hundreds turned from him each day. But the day in Bethany raised my hope again for a brief moment. There he raised Lazarus from the dead, healed the sick and the wounded, and the people thronged about him as of old, but he spoke again of love among the sons of men.

We gathered at the house of Simon to eat and drink when the day was done. But there he seemed a humble servant, not a conquering king. After we had eaten, Mary came with ointment, precious ointment, too, and poured it on his feet. It made me sick to see such waste. I was hard put to pay our way and feed the poor, and feed the poor I must, for they would rise and fight for him. With angry words I denounced the foolish act. But Jesus smiled and bade me hold my tongue. He must have known his end was near for he placed his hand upon my arm and said, "The poor ye have always with you, but my time is near."

I left him then, determined I would force his hand. I would betray him into the hands of the Pharisees and force the fight I knew must come. With his legions of angels we would win the world for God. I found the scheming Annas, and told him he might take Jesus before the week had passed. I would lead him to the secret place where Jesus prayed at night.

On the morrow, the Master rode into Jerusalem. I joined him at the gate. The people, thinking he had come to proclaim himself their king, sang hosannas and laid palm branches in his path. Eagerly I whispered in his ear, "Master, now is the time." But with a gentle smile he turned to me to say, "Judas, my dear friend, you do not understand."

He went directly to the temple where throngs were gathered for the festive day. Fury burned in his eyes when he saw the trading in the temple court. Greedy money-changers made the pilgrims pay to the last farthing for their doves to sacrifice. They cheated and they lied as they plied their ugly trade. What a scene he caused. Advancing with a whip, the Master drove them out, "This is my father's house," he cried, "and ye have made it a den of thieves." They quailed and fled before his righteous wrath and the people cheered his nerve. And then, without another word, he turned and went away to pray.

The week is a nightmare, now, my sister. The agony, suspense and fear were almost more than I could bear. Only yesterday he told us to meet him in the Upper Room as soon as the sun went down. When we had gathered there he did a gracious deed that nearly broke my heart and turned me from my traitorous plan. He came with towel and basin, and he, a king, washed our tired, dusty feet.

When we had gathered at the table, it seemed as if he honored me. He bade me sit upon his left with John upon the right. He took the bread and passed it to us all, and then he prayed as never man prayed before. My blood ran cold when he prayed for me. As he took the bread, he broke it saying, "This is my body, broken for you." I see it now, he would die to make us understand the truth. He would throw away his life to save us from our selfish selves. He would give himself to prove the power of love.

Then he took a cup of wine, and once again he prayed. "This is my blood," he said, "which is shed for you, for the remission of sins." I wondered then in cold terror, if I had been all wrong. What if he should not proclaim his Kingdom when the soldiers came to take him? What if he should choose again the way of love and let his blood drip red from a cross?

His next words made my heart stand still. I could not believe my ears. Quietly he announced, with sorrow in his voice, "One of you will betray me." Twelve pairs of eyes turned quickly to his face. Twelve voices seemed to say as one, "Master, is it I?" How could he know what I had done? How could he dream that I alone was false? But his whisper came back as low as mine so none of the others might hear: "Thou hast said." My heart beat fast and my face burned red. He spoke again with quiet words, "What thou doest, Judas Iscariot, do thou quickly."

I arose from the table and strode from the room. Angry and chagrined, I hurried to the house of Annas. I found him there and bade him make ready to go to the garden of Gethsemane where I knew Jesus intended to go. He called his servants and the soldiers and soon we were on our way.

I was half eager, half afraid. If only Jesus would show his power and proclaim his reign. If only he would call the hosts of God to crush our enemies and set us free from Rome. The priests and Pharisees were jubilant. They would make an example of this foolish impostor. They would see him nailed to a cross and broken before the world.

The soldiers led the way, their torches lighting the garden and casting weird shadows all about. Then I saw Jesus. He advanced to meet us unafraid, Peter and John at his side. "Whom seek ye?" he asked as I strode forward and placed a dreadful kiss upon his cheek. The chief priest spoke in a brazen voice, "We seek Jesus of Nazareth." "I am he," the Master answered without a trace of fear. "Take him," the priest commanded. But Peter, my courageous friend, drew his sword as if to fight alone. Hope flamed in my soul for a moment and then it was crushed. The old familiar spirit which I had known so long put an end to all my dreams. The Master spoke again, "Put up thy sword into thy sheath, Simon Peter. Shall I not drink of the cup my Father hath given me?"

Sick of heart I turned and fled out into the night. I wandered through the darkness, fell upon my knees, and prayed until my soul began to see. I heard his soft-spoken words anew, "This new commandment give I unto you, that ye love one another, even as I have loved you." He loved me, that I know. When my heart was black with traitorous plans, he washed my feet. When he knew I would betray him, he bade me sit beside him at the feast. When he saw that I would go, he gave no sign to save himself, but let me go in peace.

When I returned from praying in the night, I sought again the priests. I took them back their silver bribe and begged them to let him go. But they laughed and mocked me until I hurled their filthy coins upon the floor and fled again into the night.

What can I do? How can I face the world again with my false betrayal upon my heavy heart? Thinkest thou that Jesus would forgive me? Yes, I am sure he would, but oh, my God, I can't forgive myself.

THE MAN WHO CHALLENGED
CUSTOM

This man ceaseth not to speak blasphemous words against this holy place, and the law: for we have heard him say, that this Jesus of Nazareth shall destroy this place, and shall change the customs which Moses delivered unto us.

ACTS 6:13

STEPHEN WAS A DEACON, THE FIRST OF SEVEN TO BE SELECTED BY THE early church to minister to the needy. He was "a man full of faith and of the Holy Ghost." Obviously he took his duties seriously. Being a deacon involved far more for him than simply accepting the honor of an office. He not only ministered to the poor, but he also took a positive stand for Christian principle. That is why he became the first Christian martyr. Since he was committed as a Christian to follow his Lord, he challenged the customs and conventions of Judaism at the points where he felt them to be un-Christian.

I

It is important to notice, however, that Stephen's challenge to the religious customs of Judaism stemmed from a thorough knowledge of the past. When the leaders of the Jerusalem synagogue complained that they had heard Stephen say Jesus of Nazareth "shall change the customs which Moses delivered unto us," Stephen re-

plied with an astonishing recital of Israel's history from Abraham
to the prophets. He knew as much about Moses as the Pharisees
and what he did not know about the history of his people was
hardly worth knowing. In all probability if he had known less he
would have lived longer. It is easy to discredit and dismiss a crack-
pot who merely speaks off the top of an empty head. But Stephen
could not be discredited. According to the record, the leaders of the
synagogue "were not able to resist the wisdom and spirit by which
he spoke." He knew what he knew and his enemies knew that he
knew. Therefore, they stoned him to silence him. In their blindness,
they would not change their ways.

It is a good thing to challenge custom and to re-examine the shape
of things as they are, but change is perilous without some sense of
the flow of history. We need to be reminded that

> The old order changeth, yielding place to new;
> And God fulfils himself in many ways,
> Lest one good custom should corrupt the world.

Nevertheless, whether God fulfills Himself in change depends upon
the direction of the change. Hitler changed things, but God did not
fulfill Himself in the Nazi revolt against civilized traditions. Stalin
changed things, but God is not fulfilling Himself in Communist
tyranny. Change may very well take us backward instead of forward. Therefore, unless like Stephen we challenge custom in the
light of historic experience we may very well go the wrong way.

Every man has a right to make mistakes and to go the wrong
way, and most of us avail ourselves of that right. However, there
are some mistakes we do not need to make. Of course, we have to
learn, but we need to remember that there are two ways of learning.
We can learn by the experience of others. We do not need to try
everything at once and then wish we had not. If we have good sense
we do not try all the sins in the devil's catalogue to see for ourselves
whether the Ten Commandments make sense. We can learn from

the experience of others. But if we want to be stubborn and stupid, we can learn "the hard way." Like the rebellious college sophomore, we can "challenge everything and try everything." We can flaunt all customs and defy all traditions in the name of freedom and pay the price, learning by way of pain and suffering.

Too often we think we are blazing new trails when in reality we are floundering along an old trail, long since overgrown with timber and brush. You would think there never had been paternalistic governments, generous enough to support the people with their own money. Nothing could be further from the truth. Rome got that way just before her fall. Toward the end her leaders stayed in power with free grain and free circuses, and every pretender to power shouted, "I can do it better." The time came when Rome was a pushover for the vigorous barbarians who were not civilized enough to believe in something for nothing. So whenever you challenge the social and economic habits of a nation it is important to learn as much as possible from history.

There are not a few people who seem to think that by advocating free love, companionate marriage and sex where you find it, they are pioneering new ground. They think that by challenging conventions and moral customs they are thoroughly modern and up-to-date. As a matter of fact, they are several thousand years behind the time, blundering along an old trail that led nowhere at all. Free love was old before Sampson blundered into Delilah. Humanity had to learn by a long and bitter experience that there is nothing so rewarding as one man and one woman loving each other so much that they have no wish to love any other. Of course, you are free to learn the hard way if you wish. You can discard the customs and conventions of civilized society if you please, but not in the name of progress. It is retrogression, if history has any meaning at all.

There is another area in which people seem to think they are pioneers, emancipating their times from the relative sobriety of the prohibition era. If you listen much to the radio it must seem alto-gether clear that good beer is our new Messiah. It will cure anything from sadness to anemia. It's wonderful for what ails you. Or, if you want something stronger, of course "Clear heads drink Calvert" and then are not clear any more. If you have switched lately, I'd advise a switch back to Coca Cola. Your head will be clearer. Noah made a fool of himself back in the days of the flood. According to the Scriptures, "Noah was drunk," and there is no record anywhere of anybody getting anything but a befuddled head or a headache from following in Noah's footsteps.

When you get ready to challenge a custom or a convention, there is no sense in leading with your chin. You will make plenty of mistakes even if you learn much from the experience of history. You don't need to learn everything the hard way.

II

Following in the footsteps of his Lord, Stephen had the wisdom to see the difference between the sound and the unsound in the customs of his people, between what Jesus called "the law of God" and "the traditions of men." There was the matter of Sabbath ob-servance. The rules were explicit and too numerous for anybody to remember. No work whatever was to be done on the Sabbath. You could not eat an egg a hen laid on the Sabbath and if you wore false teeth on the Sabbath you broke the law against bearing a burden on the holy day. If you dug in your garden on the Sabbath you were liable to stoning. You could not reap on the Sabbath and a woman was not allowed to use a mirror on the Sabbath, for if she did she might see a gray hair and pull it out, and pulling out gray hairs was reaping.

It is important, of course, to "remember the Sabbath day to keep it holy," but it is also important to note that "the Sabbath was made for man, not man for the Sabbath," as Jesus said. Custom had to be judged by what it did to people. If customs made men cheat, lie, deceive, the customs were wrong. If customs did nothing to enrich life and make it more meaningful, they were unimportant. If customs merely made life burdensome, they were not "the law of God." Customs were to be judged by what they did to the physical, moral and spiritual life of people.

The problem of life is to discriminate, to sense the difference between "the things that cannot be shaken" because they are rooted in "the law of God" and the things that can be shaken because they merely are "the traditions of men." It is interesting to observe that in 1847 when Karl Marx and Friedrich Engels published their *Communist Manifesto* they challenged not a few of the customs of capitalist society that needed to be challenged. They challenged the conventional assumption that the rich had a right to rule. They disputed the idea that the workers are a permanently inferior class. They denied the right of the powerful to own the weak, body, mind and soul. They defied the assumption that workers were no more than cogs in an economic machine, to be cast aside in the end like worn-out machinery.

Unhappily, Marx and Engels threw out the baby with the bath. They wanted to throw out the whole system. They did not even see the values in it, the freedom, the initiative, the progress it could promote. It never occurred to them that evil customs which had attached themselves to the capitalist system might be modified or eliminated, and it never entered their heads that the system they proposed might turn out to have more potential evils in it than the system they condemned. You don't throw out the Sabbath day just because a few people insist on the wrong observance of it. On the contrary, you discriminate, and remember the Sabbath in such a way that it may be physically, morally and spiritually creative. So in the capitalistic system. It has been misused. It has been careless of human values. It has ridden roughshod over moral ideals. It has inspired a materialistic philosophy of unenlightened selfishness. But so has every other system known to history. Nevertheless, in the hands of some great Christians I have known I think it has been an expression of Christianity at its best. In the hands of Christian men, who dare to challenge unchristian customs, capitalism can be morally and spiritually creative.

What bothers me is not capitalism as a system, but rather the fact that there are too few Christians who will challenge unchristian customs that have attached themselves to the system. There is the habit of exaggeration and misrepresentation for the sake of a profit. It is not Christian. There is the emphasis on wages, hours and profits, with too little on common welfare and community service. There is too little concern for individual employees, too much that is hard fisted and impersonal. There is too much seeking of unfair advantage by way of economic power or government favor. God give us men who will "change the customs" which have attached themselves to our system, men who will see the difference between "the law of God and the tradition of men."

III

When Stephen faced the unsound customs that had attached themselves to the core of Judaism, he had the courage to speak his mind. He might very well have avoided difficult issues and simply stuck to the simple gospel. He did not need to challenge the corrupt legalism of Judaism. He might have soft pedaled his conviction that the Messiah had come in Jesus. He did not need to tell the Pharisees they had crucified and ignored their prophets in the name of their conventional religion. If he had been content to keep still he might have lived a long and comfortable life. Stephen had a priceless quality called courage. He was a follower of one whose courage took him to the cross.

Every time humanity has struck its tents and marched forward, some man of courage has taken the lead, striking at the shackles of enslaving customs. There was Martin Luther, striking away the chains of spiritual bondage imposed by a church that had grown powerful and corrupt. There was Voltaire, challenging the custom of tyranny in the name of freedom under God. There was Lord Shaftesbury, defying the tradition of child labor, and John Howard striking off the chains of men imprisoned for debt. There was Wendell Phillips, hurling his strength against the custom of human slavery. The weight of power was against them, but sheer courage won the day. They were villified and threatened and persecuted, but they said what they had to say. They would not be clams for the sake of safety and security.

In all probability no living creature has such a strong guarantee of security as the clam. All he has to do to get nourishment is to open his doors and food comes in. He hides comfortably in his shell safe from danger, secure from attack. He has no neck to stick out or risk. He simply lives. On the other hand, the eagle lives a hazardous life. He builds his nest on rocky crags and takes his life in his hands every time he swoops down to the earth for food. He has to be challenging the elements around him from dawn until dark, beating the winds with his wings, defying storms, overcoming the cold. Having seen an eagle, who wants to be a clam? Maybe that is why we have made the eagle the symbol of our nation.

Curiously enough, we Christians have become more like clams than eagles. We do not wish to soar above the customs that ought to be changed in the name of Christ. We feel a little as Charles felt about Joan of Arc in Bernard Shaw's play, when Charles, nearly distracted, said: "Why doesn't she shut up or go home?" No doubt the Pharisees felt that way about Jesus. Mentally and spiritually he soared above the confining customs of his time. He would not shut up. He would not stay put like a clam. He was forever saying: "Ye have heard it said of olden time . . . but I say unto you," challenging custom and changing conventions.

But we, who are his followers, have turned into clams, and nothing will be changed if we are silent. Who wants to change the habit of government inefficiency and graft? Certainly not those who profit by it. Who wants to change the custom of race discrimination? Certainly not those who are satisfied with it. Who wants to change the custom of settling disputes by violence? Certainly not those who are untroubled by social disintegration. Who wants to change the custom of scorning spiritual values in the name of realism? Certainly not those who feel no desperate spiritual need.

It takes courage to challenge custom, to say what we think and then march off in new directions, but courage is the hinge on the door to the future. Stephen, the man who challenged custom for the sake of his Lord, lost his life in the bargain, but he left a mark the ages cannot erase. Nobody ever remembered a clam with a monument, or elected a clam to be a saint. Nobody ever erected a church in honor of St. Clam.

IV

Obviously, the men and women who like Stephen have challenged custom in the name of Christ have been men and women whose courage was rooted in faith. There is a stirring truth in the Greek drama *Antigone* in which a gallant woman rebelled against a custom of the state. Antigone's brother had been a traitor to his city, and in his treacherous war had lost his life. By order of the city's governor his body was left to rot, unburied—as fit indignity for his baseness. But Antigone was resolved to give her brother a decent burial. There was a law of love deeper than the shame of treachery and higher than the custom of the state. So she also was condemned to die for disobedience, and to die by starvation. Seeing her inflexible, the governor asked:

"And didst thou dare to disobey these laws?" She answered him:

> I did not dream thine edict strong enough
> That thou, a mortal man, shoulds't overpass
> The unwritten laws of God that know no change.

"The unwritten laws of God that know no change"! Jesus broke with man-made customs, not that he might be a roving meteor, but that he might move in the orbit of an Eternal Will. He soared above the customs and traditions of men in obedience to his faith in the rightness and the love of God. We never will move beyond today to the promise of tomorrow without faith to undergird our courage.

There is a striking story coming out of the French Revolution, with its violence and terror. Louis XVI, Marie Antoinette and the little dauphin, inside the palace, had listened to the teeming roar of the rebellious mob outside. Windows had been smashed, and stones hurled. On the morrow the mob came back, and the little dauphin turned to his mother to ask: "Mama, is it still yesterday?" It always will be yesterday until, like Stephen, we challenge the unchristian customs of our time in the name of Jesus Christ Our Lord.

ONE CROWDED HOUR
OF LIFE

In him was life; and the life was the light of men.

JOHN 1:4

T HE CLOUDS HAD BEEN DARK OVER CALVARY THROUGH THE EARLY afternoon, but now the setting sun illuminated a hill shaped like a human skull. Two men, dressed in garments that suggested both wealth and prominence, tenderly lowered a blood-stained body from a Roman cross and wrapped it in a linen winding sheet. They began, then, the difficult descent to a garden at the foot of a rocky path. They paused before a new and open tomb, uttered a prayer and hastily placed the body in the tomb. They dared not tarry, for the sun was on the horizon, and with the sunset came the Sabbath when no Jew could touch the dead.

Evening fell quietly over the garden of Joseph of Arimathea, and a Roman guard paced back and forth before the tomb, now closed by a heavy stone at its door. Then it was dark. Bats and owls came from their haunts and screeched to one another. A lonely jackal lifted his head to the first evening star and howled to a nameless mate. In the city of Jerusalem discouraged men hid themselves in fear and despair, muttering to themselves: "We had thought it would be he who would redeem Israel."

The Sabbath passed. No Jew entered the garden or molested the

176

tomb. Pilate had doubled the guard and sealed the tomb with the stamp of Imperial Rome. He would have no resurrection nonsense to plague his kingdom or his sleep. Enough was enough, and he wanted no more of the Nazarene. So far as the disciples were concerned, Pilate went to a lot of trouble for nothing. Jesus was dead and that was that. As for Peter, he said: "I go a-fishing." A sentimental interlude was ended and the disciples were quite ready to pick up their lives where they had left off at the Master's call. Then it happened. Jesus was not dead; he was gloriously alive. He would be with them always, and under the spell of his living spirit eleven defeated, disillusioned men were transformed into men of power. They marched out into their world with heads erect and eyes alight to be "more than conquerors" in the Master's name.

I

That crowded hour of Easter dawn was a watershed of history. In that baffling hour of resurrection, God invaded human history to affirm the endless sovereignty of Christ through time and tide. In one staggering event God snatched from human hands the victory won by naked power and set the goal of human striving in the high calling of Christian discipleship. There in the garden of Joseph of Arimathea God laid the touchstone of human progress, by which events and movements are measured. In the words of John, God affirmed that "in him was life; and the life was the light of men."

We cannot escape Jesus Christ as the touchstone of human progress. He invades both life and history to measure the meaning of events. What we call progress is no more than meaningless motion unless it is movement toward the mind of Christ. Every step we take along the road from birth to death has somewhere its relation to the living Christ. Every event of history stands in judgment before his mind and spirit. Events are fraught with good or ill as they relate to him. Over and over again in history God confronts us with the imperative: "This is my beloved Son, in whom I am well pleased. Hear ye him."

There have been many crowded hours of destiny along the corridors of time. There have been occasions when the past has been sucked into the whirling vortex of the present to change "the shape of things to come." There have been times when eternity has been poured into one hour. Now and then something new and decisive enters history and whether we wish or no, we have to reckon with it. To be sure, there may have been years, even centuries of preparation for the decisive event. Usually that is the case. But there comes an hour when newness crowds our lives with shattering impact. Always, however, when the event occurs, it stands in judgment before Jesus Christ.

Let me suggest in concrete terms what I mean. Some time ago I dropped into a movie. It was a double feature, a survey of the twenties and a western. I am not sure which intrigued me most, though I suspect the western had priority. The story of the twenties was just beginning as I found a seat. I watched Gertrude Ederle swimming the English Channel. I saw Jack Dempsey in his famous fight with Gene Tunney, and I watched Sacco and Vanzetti going on trial. Then came the decisive moment. An unknown young man named Charles Lindbergh raced down a runway of Roosevelt Field in New York in a plane called *The Spirit of St. Louis*. My mind went back to my own memory of that event. It was a thrilling time and the whole nation waited anxiously for word of Lindbergh's progress. Then, on the screen, I watched him land in Paris.

History crowded into that hour when Lindbergh landed, the first man to fly the Atlantic from New York to Paris. In one momentous hour the world became one world. A collection of discrete and separate worlds became a neighborhood. We did not know it then, but that event took us back across the centuries to the garden of Joseph of Arimathea, for it presented us with a fateful choice between one world in Christ, or none. We were not aware of it then, but that crowded hour of destiny carried us back to another hour when God invaded history to say: "This is my beloved son. . . . Hear ye him." In the hour when Lindbergh landed in Paris we faced a choice between life and death for the world. In that hour the words of John had decisive meaning for us all: "In him was life; and the life was the light of men."

In your lifetime and mine there was another crowded hour, when eternity invaded time. News of it came to me hours after the event. I was on a camping trip and I had just finished making a bed of pine boughs in the shadow of Mt. Neva, high in the Colorado Rockies. A passing ranger brought the news of Nagasaki and Hiroshima. Atomic bombs had fallen, and the ranger said with undisguised enthusiasm: "We really cooked 'em. The war will be over in no time now." That night I went out and sat on a gnarled stump in a little valley where the Arapahoe Indians once held their powwows. A century or so before a few braves had fought other braves with bows and arrows and nobody cared too much. Now it was different. Something new and decisive had come into history, and never again would life be the same. Nagasaki and Hiroshima were strange words with a faraway sound there in my little valley with stars shining overhead and a tinkling stream making music beside me, yet they were freighted with significance. Something new had burst upon the world and once again we were confronted with a choice.

Life came to the world like a shining light in the garden of Joseph of Arimathea; death came with a shroud at Nagasaki and Hiroshima. Caesar and Genghis Khan, Napoleon and Bismarck, Hitler and Mussolini paled into insignificance when the fury of the atom was released. A new factor entered history and for the first time it was clear that man possessed the means of his own destruction. Now it is not a question of Christ or chaos. We have the chaos now. It is rather a question of Christ or final catastrophe. There is no use talking about one more war to save the world. With one more war there will be nothing to save.

We are back again beside the tomb of Christ at Easter dawn, standing in the judgment of his resurrection. "In him was life; and the life was the light of men," and we will have to choose. We can give ourselves into the hands of a military bureaucracy and stake our fortunes on naked force, if we please. But we had better remember that Christ stands in judgment now as then. Progress is in him, and death in Caesar. Nothing that we do or say can change that truth, for God Himself has spoken.

II

Let it be noted, too, that God invaded history that Easter dawn to set the touchstone for the progress of our private lives. Our progress, too, depends on hearing him who died to live again. We cannot measure our progress by place or position, by our neighbors or even by our self-estimate. We stand in judgment before the open tomb. Day by day we choose to be or not to be what God intended. We hear the word, "In him was life; and the life was the light of men," and we choose life and light or darkness and death.

In individual life as in history there are crowded hours when time and eternity meet. Time confronts us with decisions, throws us into situations that are arbiters of our destiny, and we set the course of our lives. I was startled by a newspaper headline not long ago. It was on the sports page and it headed the story of colleges clamoring for high school football stars. The headline read: "'WHAT'S IN IT FOR ME?' HIGH SCHOOL ATHLETES ASK." "What's in it for me?" In those words I found the answer to basketball's fixed games, to Frank Costello and a host of lesser gamblers on the public scene. In those words I found the answer to the shoddy ways of Washington and the politicians who pervert their public trust.

Our trouble lies in the fact we are asking the wrong question. When God invaded history He posed a deeper question for our souls. The question is: "What's in it that lasts?" That is but an-other way of asking: "What's in it that squares with the mind of Christ?" You see, life grows and moves toward greatness only by feeding on the things that last. A Canadian aviator put the matter straight in a novel called *Fresh Wind Blowing*. Just before he set off on a fatal bombing mission he wrote to his wife: "Accept the thought of death for yourself and for others. Then go on living as richly and adventurously as you can, holding fast to the things death cannot touch." So, the final question in every decision is: "What's in it that death cannot touch?"

God made it clear that first Easter dawn that the mind of Christ in us is all there is to last, all there is death cannot touch. "In him was life; and the life was the light of men." Hell is not a place, it is a condition, a condition of character in which there is nothing to last. Heaven is not a place, it is a condition wherein the mind of Christ has come to dwell in us. That is what Oscar Wilde tried to say in his story of the sinner standing in the judgment hall before God. God says with a touch of sadness: "I'll have to send you to hell." The answer comes back from the depths of pain: "You can't send me to hell. I'm there already." There is silence, then, and angels, startled, look toward God. At last God speaks again: "Then I'll send you to heaven." But the answer comes once more: "You can't send me to heaven. I've never been able to imagine it."

You cannot imagine heaven unless you have known and cher-ished things "death cannot touch." You cannot possibly imagine heaven with nothing but shoddy things inside, with nothing in mind but the question: "What's in it for me?" So, as Emerson said: "Every day is doom's day." Every hour is crowded with life or death, for in every hour we make decisive choices. We choose be-tween love that lasts, and lust that dies. We choose between truth that stands forever, and lies that flounder. We choose between good-ness that is permanent, and evil that is transient. Little by little we are "growing up in all things unto him who is the head," or we are spending much too much for too little.

Perhaps we ought to note in passing that the choices we make in the crowded hours when time and eternity meet in history flow from the choices we have made in personal life. History, as Arnold Toynbee notes, is but the reflection of the struggles of the souls of men. What goes on in Washington is but a reflection of our common life. What happens in the counsels of the nation is but an echo of the littleness or greatness in us. As a nation we never will stand strongly for the "things death cannot touch" until those things are strong in us. Life crowds us now, crowds us to decide, and yet we know: "In him was life; and the life was the light of men."

III

The crowning note of Easter is the note of triumph and of hope, for in the resurrection the love of God invaded history. With the eloquence of an empty tomb God offered His redeeming love to us. Though we crucify Him day by day, His love remains as steady as the stars. Ever and anon He comes to us in crowded hours of choice, waiting with endless patience for us to answer with our lives. There is a hint of the truth in a modern novel wherein a worthless husband makes a shambles of a home. He is shiftless and unfaithful, brutal and disgusting. A whole community is against him, and his wife's family would have the law on him. But says Mary in the story: "I know he's no good, but I love him. Maybe if I stick by him he'll turn out all right in the end."

Sometimes I wonder if we are any of us much good in God's eyes. The best of us are blundering fools. We are selfish and stubborn and belligerent. We are so busy feathering our own nests we don't really care a plugged nickel about the kingdom of God. I wonder sometimes why God loves us at all. Somebody asked Bernard Shaw once who he would pick among the great men and women on the earth to start a new dispensation if he could be Noah in another flood. The old patriarch flashed back: "I'd let 'em all drown." Well, maybe Shaw would, but God wouldn't.

God keeps loving with a patience beyond anything we know of patience. And now and then in crises of decision we answer God's love and go another road. Now and then we take His hand, perhaps in tears, and find a crowded, wonderful hour of life that marks our turning and redemption. Once in a hundred years a St. Francis, a Wesley, a Gandhi answers the love of God with such devotion that history is altered and for a while new paths are charted.

Possibly the crisis of the present hour will lead us to a turning; I am not sure. It could happen that we will be caught up in a new Pentecost, answering the love of God with great devotion and with irresistible power. Jesus suggested as much once in a terrifying parable. We call it the little apocalypse. The picture he painted was grim, but we can understand it. He said that "nation shall rise against nation and kingdom against kingdom." There shall be "famine and pestilence" and "great distress in the land." "And there shall be signs in the sun, and moon and stars; and upon the earth distress of nations with perplexity." In the midst of all this "men fainting for fear, and for expectation of the things which are coming on the world: for the powers of the heavens shall be shaken."

What then? Is the end doom and death? Is the end hopeless from the beginning? Not so, says Jesus, for "when these things begin to come to pass, then look up, and lift up your heads; for your redemption draweth nigh." So, when things look darkest and our follies have led us to the chasm of disaster, there still is a chance if we claim it. God's love never ceases. Maybe we will answer and begin living now for the things "death cannot touch." Maybe we will "look up, and lift up our heads," believing that "in him was life; and the life was the light of men."

ANOTHER MILE BEYOND

❦

===

And whosoever shall compel thee to go a mile, go with
him twain.   MATTHEW 5:41

⥣

YOUR LIFE IS A COMPOSITE OF THE THINGS YOU MUST DO AND THE
things you voluntarily choose to do. There are obligations you
are compelled to accept and responsibilities you assume because you
wish to do so. Young people go to school because they must, but
they play football and assume responsibilities for training and practice because they want to play football. You work at your job because you must in order to live, but you spend endless hours doing
committee work for your clubs because you find pleasure or satisfaction in so doing. The problem of life, as Jesus saw it, is to transform the necessary into the voluntary; to do what you must as if
you would rather do it than anything else.

Jesus pointed up his thinking about the matter in a simple sentence: "Whosoever shall compel thee to go a mile, go with him
twain." It should be noted that Jesus was addressing himself to a
specific problem of his contemporaries. A Roman on imperial business could require a Jew to carry his burden one mile in any direction, and the Romans, you may be sure, made the most of the
privilege. The Jews were bitterly resentful. Jesus did not defend the
custom, not for a moment, but he offered a formula for dealing
creatively with an unpleasant necessity. He suggested a way of tak-

ing the sting out of coercion by making it voluntary. He would not do less than was required, but more. The second mile was the testament of a man's freedom, and a denial of his slavery.

I

The philosophy of the second mile relates to your life and to mine and bears decisively on our daily experience. We are perpetually in the position of having to do what we would rather not. Life says we must go here or there, do this or that, and we resent the "musts." A discerning lad put our feeling in a nutshell when he said to his mother, "Mom, please don't say 'must,' it makes me feel 'won't' all over." So it is with us. When life says you must, you feel won't all over. When life imposes unwanted demands, we often seethe with resentment, like a Jew bearing the burden of a Roman along a dusty road.

The normal reaction to a "must" to which our feelings say "won't" is a grudging performance. We do what we must, but not even a shade more. We slide through on a bare minimum. When a small girl is told she must wash the dishes, the normal question is: "Do I have to put them away, too?" When a boy is admonished to cut the lawn, he wants to know: "Do I have to cut both the front yard and the back?" The student, assigned a paper to write, wants to know: "How long does it have to be? Do the typewriter pages have to be single spaced or can they be double spaced?"

Sometimes I am persuaded that we greet life with what might be called the minimum mind. When we meet the "musts" we answer with the minimum average. Look out for that word "average," it is the refuge of the minimum mind. At Evanston High School, or any other high school for that matter, a grade of four is average. I am inclined to suspect, however, that a four grade is not the average in actual capacity. It is the average in production very largely because the minimum mind is quite content to be average. The minimum mind says, "If I must, I must, but I won't hurt myself."

Unhappily, our whole society competes against the average. The workman who lays bricks competes against the average. He does not work at full capacity, no; he works at a minimum average. Of course, when you focus on the average, you are bound to level things down, not up. The average inevitably gets lower, not higher, and anyone who goes the second mile is distinctly unpopular. Now and then I receive through the mail blanks requesting information about somebody who wants a job. The blanks are very much alike. They want to know whether so and so is "above average, average, below average." Well, it is no compliment to be "average," and heaven help anybody who is "below average." The average is the minimum not the maximum. There is none of the second mile in it.

Take the matter of giving to the church or the community chest. Giving seems to be a "must" to which a considerable number of minds say "won't" and then compromise with the minimum. It may be necessary, but there is no fun in it. So, we dig around to find out what is "average." Of course we rationalize our minimum by saying: "If I give too much I will be doing more than my share. Somebody else will shirk." Reason is a skillful pleader when she is enlisted in the service of the minimum mind. She can find good reasons for sticking to the average and decisive reasons for keeping to the minimum. The philosophy of the second mile has not caught on yet in any telling way.

In our homes the minimum mind plays havoc with our happiness. We give too little to the life of our homes and we give it too late. We are satisfied with the average. I remember a young woman who complained bitterly, "My husband is always telling me he is a better husband than most of his acquaintances." Maybe so, but love is not interested in averages. What the average husband does is a miserable standard for judgment. Judging by divorce statistics, the average is nowhere near good enough. It takes the second mile to make a home a pleasant place. The minimum mind is fatal at home.

You cannot live richly anywhere with a minimum mind. Every

time life confronts you with a "must" you will rear up with a "won't" and then compromise with a grudging average. You will be crabby and irritable and sometimes resentful because life seems too demanding. You will be a slave to sheer drudgery, not a free man full of zest for the second mile you give for the sheer fun of it. If you want life, real life, I mean, you will have to go another mile beyond sheer necessity. So, "Whosoever shall compel thee to go a mile, go with him twain."

II

It is plain that the minimum mind is altogether normal in our time. It is evidence of human nature not really touched by the mind of Christ. It is not lavish, or generous, or enthusiastic with a dash of the divine in it. On the contrary, it is sluggish and bored and resentful, just plodding along in a rut. By way of contrast, the mind committed to the maximum is a thrilling thing. God is in it, overflowing into life as He did at Calvary. He is in the life and the joy that flow from the second mile.

There is a hint of what I mean in the comment of Miss Booth, whose father founded the Salvation Army. Through the years she worked along with her father, sacrificing the things she wanted for the sake of her father's dream; going the second mile when anybody would have told her one mile was more than enough. At eighty, when she looked back over the years, she had no regrets. As she put it, "every sacrifice has had its halo." Oh yes, she went on to add, "Each sacrifice has had its tears, has aroused doubts, has claimed its price, but it has always had its halo." It is the halos we miss when our minds are committed to the minimum, the inner glow that makes us feel good all over.

You don't feel so good when you shirk your duties and coast along just average. There is no lift in drudgery, and any job or task is drudgery if you are doing it purely because you must. Any sacrifice is too much to be accepted if it is imposed and you have no choice. But you can change the complexion of anything you have to do or endure if you can substitute a maximum mind for a minimum mind. There is no halo in anything you do until you get beyond the average to the extra. There is no thrill in giving until you give a maximum that costs you something. You will be bored to death on your job until you get around to giving your maximum, that extra that is not reflected in your pay envelope.

There is a striking story in the New Testament that suggests what I mean by the maximum mind. It concerns the Rich Young Ruler who came to Jesus eager to inherit eternal life. He assured the Master he had kept the commandments. He was not in the habit of bearing false witness. He had not committed adultery. He never had defrauded anybody and he honored his father and his mother. In short, he was most respectable in a minimum way. When Jesus said to him, "Go, sell all thou hast, and give to the poor," the young man was frightfully upset, for as the record notes, "he had great possessions."

The moral of the story is not that we should give away everything we possess and join a monastic order. Even a monastic order would be in a bad way if there were not some people on the outside able and willing to give something to keep the monastery going. The trouble with the Rich Young Ruler was that he had a mind committed to the minimum. He lived by the rules, but not beyond them: he was obedient to the obligatory, but not moved by the maximum. He wanted to inherit eternal life on his own minimum terms. He wanted a halo without exorbitant expense.

A mind committed to the maximum can transform unwanted duties into redeeming satisfactions. Take our in-law duties, for example. Maybe your father-in-law died, and when that happened you went the second mile and invited your mother-in-law to live in your home. Actually, it was not a whole two-mile affair. There did not seem to be anything else you could do. As of now, things are a bit rugged. You are doing your duty by your mother-in-law. You will not let her starve, and you will not lock her out in the rain. But your mind is committed to the minimum, and life is more hell than halo. It takes the spirit of the second mile to transform an in-law problem into a triumph. Browning had the key to the transformation when he wrote:

> The little more, and how much it is,
> The little less, and what worlds away.

It is the little more that marks the second mile and leads to joy at home or anywhere else.

III

At the secular level where most of us live most of the time, the whole idea of going another mile beyond the necessary seems like nonsense. It does not make sense until life is committed to something. Somebody noted once that genius is simply "the transcendent capacity for taking trouble." But it should be observed that the genius is always committed to something in whose service he takes trouble. He is dedicated to science, to art, to music, to business, and he gives more of himself to his particular art than anyone would have a right to demand. He takes pains beyond the ordinary and goes to no end of trouble for the sake of his art.

The simple truth is you cannot go the second mile simply on your own steam. George Small had it right when he wrote, "I read in a book that a man called Christ went about doing good. It is very disconcerting to me that I am so easily satisfied with just going about." So we are satisfied "just going about" quite forgetting the significance of the second mile until we get around to a great dedication of ourselves to something big enough to make us lose sight of ourselves.

The only thing I know that will take us the second mile with any consistency is what might be called noncalculating love. You can see it in Jesus. He was forever doing the unexpected, the surprising, going beyond the usual, throwing in something extra. He said it was God's way, not his, and his whole life suggests that it is God's nature to give you more than you expect, more than you ask for. There is nothing coldly calculating about the love of God. It is a wholehearted thing. It gives you more than legal good measure. It offers forgiveness you have no right to expect, and strength you do not deserve, and serenity you cannot demand.

There is a suggestion of God's noncalculating love in what we see around us. You plant seeds in the earth and you get back not just what you planted. You get back a hundredfold more than you planted. God wraps His apple seeds in wonderful juicy fruit, and it is all thrown in extra for good measure. Rufus Jones reminds us of an old Chinese proverb to the effect that any fool can count the number of seeds in an apple but nobody can count the number of apples in an apple seed. It just keeps on producing more seeds and more trees and more apples beyond counting. There is nothing niggardly about the love of God. It is lavish and generous beyond any notion we have of generosity.

The Christian faith insists that the maximum mind, pushing on another mile beyond what is necessary, is our response to the love of God poured out supremely on an "old rugged cross." When we love Him because He first loved us, the mood of the second mile gets into our blood stream. We give up asking in the face of every demand, "What's in it for me?" We know full well we already have had more than we had any right to ask or think. We could spend a lifetime serving the highest and giving our best to life and not give back a tenth of what God has given.

Sometimes, however, I think we are a little like our children. We love them no end. We sacrifice and save and struggle to get them through college, and sometimes they seem to take it all for granted. We do not love them any the less, even if they do not seem to respond with proper gratitude. We keep on loving them and doing for them, because love is noncalculating. We go on sacrificing, not with the idea that some day maybe they will support us or give us a trip to Europe, but because we love them dearly. And what do we want of them? Just their best, is all. We want them to go the second mile studying. We want them to make the most of their opportunity. Most of all, we want them to be clean and fine and loyal to the highest they know. We want them to develop character, with the mind of Christ at the center of it.

God is like that. He goes on loving and giving. There is nothing calculating about His love. We can be niggardly and selfish, stubborn and altogether ungrateful, and He goes on loving us just the same. And what does He want of us? Just a quality of life willing to go the second mile, a maximum mind in us putting our best into life. He wants in us a response, a noncalculating love, spending itself with zest and taking the luck of the road with undiscourageable good will.

Sometimes I have been troubled by the words of Scripture affirming that "the Lord thy God is a jealous God." Jealousy in God seems a little out of character, and I think it is. God really is not a green-eyed monster when you and I worship other gods, ourselves and the things we own, our business, our country or our club. He does not get mad at us and sulk. The jealousy of God is of another stripe altogether. He is jealous for us, for what we are missing, for what we are not that we could be. He is jealous because we are little, not big; petty, not large minded; he is jealous for the maximum in us and irritated by the minimum. He is jealous for us the way we are jealous for our children when they are satisfied with the minimum.

Our problem is to take life as it is and add a new dimension to it with our noncalculating love for the God who revealed Himself in Jesus Christ. When we add that new dimension the obligatory ceases to be drudgery and becomes an oblation, and we cease saying "won't" to the "must." We catch the spirit of an ancient traveler who pushed along a rugged road with a maximum mind, saying, "Whosoever shall compel thee to go a mile, go with him twain."

Set in Linotype Granjon
Format by Katharine Sitterly
Manufactured by The Haddon Craftsmen, Inc.
Published by HARPER & BROTHERS, *New York*

Date Due

DEC 16 '87			